MW01140247

>>> THE **BIG** BOOK OF <<<

OFFICE

*Bullsh*t*

First published in 2016 by Carlton Books
An imprint of the Carlton Publishing Group
20 Mortimer Street
London W1T 3JW

Copyright © Carlton Publishing Group 2016

A CIP catalogue for this book is available from the British Library.

ISBN 978-1-78097-805-5

Printed and bound by CPI Group (UK) Ltd, Croydon, CR0 4YY

10 9 8 7 6 5 4 3 2 1

HAVE THE PERFECT SICK DAY!

HILARIOUS OFFICE PRANKS

»»» THE _BIG_ BOOK OF «««

OFFICE
Bullsh*t

Hundreds of ways to waste time at work

MALCOLM CROFT

Comedy Corporate Jargon!

ANNOY YOUR BOSS WITHOUT GETTING FIRED!

CARLTON BOOKS

Dear Office Drone,

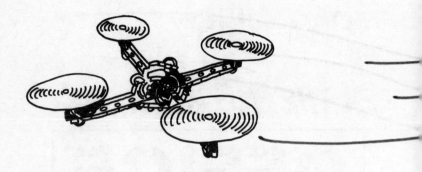

Let's be honest, office life is ridiculous. Which, I'm afraid to say, means your life is ridiculous.

You spend 40 hours a week cramped in a dank, unchallenging and unrewarding atmosphere just so you can go home at the end of a long week unsatisfied, underpaid and riddled with repetitive strain injury and pointless anxiety. So you eat. And drink. To numb the pain.

Humans, as we all know, are simply not built to sit on their butts all day, burning out our retinas staring at a spreadsheet, completely squandering the potential that more than 700 million years of glorious evolution has given us.

As the old joke goes, you work in an office for 40 years of your life – you get less for murder. Though, of course, if you work in an office, you'll have daydreamed about stapling a colleague to their desk and bludgeoning them over the head repeatedly with a QWERTY keyboard, or garroting them with a mouse cable.

So, if you're reading this at your desk, instead of working, then good for you! That's exactly what this book is about. This book is a two-fingered salute to work, a flip of the bird to The Man, and a hearty raspberry right in the face of Corporate Officedom.

If you are currently employed and show up to work at an office, if you spend the hours between nine and five sat at a cold and often cramped desk, if you are surrounded by other miserable people you

can't stand to look at, let alone talk to – you are not alone. Look to your left. That person – as annoying as they might be – is probably just as miserable as you.

By simply buying/stealing/borrowing/regifting this book, you have taken one small step into a simpler world, a world where middle managers don't exist, where computers don't need rebooting 30 times a day, where office politics is a thing that exists only in nightmares, and staff meetings are just a figment of the Devil's imagination. By admitting that you have a problem – that your office life is rubbish – we can begin to work together to solve the problem and end corporate lunacy once for and all.

Welcome to your new world order. Now, spend two hours making a cup of tea, and let's all get to work thinking about how we can leave work early tonight without anyone noticing…

● ●

Obvious Disclaimer

The publishers of this humorous book will not be held liable if you are dumb enough to actually carry out some of the dumb stuff contained within. You have been warned.

The Small print

I, the undersigned, agree that by picking up a copy of this book am taking action to demonstrate that I hate my office job – not necessarily because of the actual role I worked hard at university to qualify for, but because of the negatively charged office environment I am forced to endure day in, day out. And the incompetent idiots I must endure: their small-mindedness, arrogance and egomaniacal behaviour, and the counter-productive politics which threaten to ruin not only this company, but also all humankind in one swift death knell.

I, the undersigned, hereby reject and denounce the devil's suffocating control at [*insert your company's name here*] and, from this point on, promise to not care about staff meeting minutes, document scanning, passive/aggressive leaving cards and mindless office gossip.

Please, please make my wildest dreams come true. I cannot stand to work another second in this evil temple of doom.

_____
[*sign name here*]

Quote Quota #83

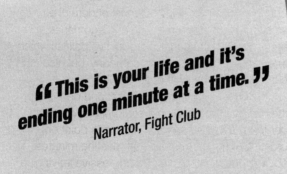

❝ This is your life and it's ending one minute at a time. ❞
Narrator, Fight Club

Lies Lies Lies

A 2014 survey of jobseekers in the UK reported how six out of
ten people admitted lying or exaggerating on their CV in order to
boost their chances of a first interview. It also reported that 16 per
cent falsely claimed to speak another language and 27 per cent
"embellished" their IT skills. Hands up… was it you?

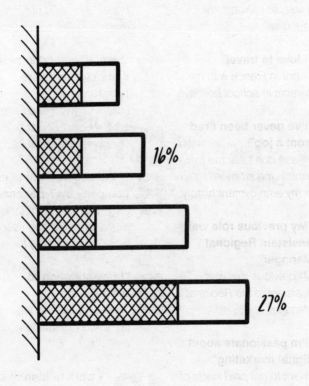

Top Ten CV Lies

We all lie on our CVs, right? Here are the most common porkies...
and their inconvenient truths:

1 **"I have a First Class degree"**
I got a 2:1, but I was one per cent away from a first, so I always just round up.

2 **"I love to travel"**
I went to France with my parents in school holidays.

3 **"I've never been fired from a job"**
Please don't ask me to explain the six-month gap in my employment history.

4 **"My previous role was Assistant Regional Manager"**
My previous role was Assistant to the Regional Manager.

5 **"I'm passionate about digital marketing"**
I want to get paid loads of money just to sit around and search Facebook all day.

6 **"I enjoy spending time with my friends and exploring the city I live in"**
I like to get drunk with my mates and hang out in as many pubs as possible.

7 **"I am advanced in most computer software programmes"**
I can use Word and Excel, a bit, the rest I'll just pick up. How hard can it be?

8 **"I increased profit at my company by 7 per cent"**
I was part of a team that reported profits had risen while I was working there.

9 **"I pay attention to the details"**
The word "details" was spelt wrong in all previous drafts of this CV.

10 **"I work brilliantly as part of a team"**
I'd sell my own mother to get this job, and screw over anyone I can to keep it.

Quote Quota #76

"Choose a job you love, and you will never have to work a day in your life."

Confucius

It Could Happen To You!

Work-related accidents result in 2.3 million fatalities around the world every year. That equates to 6,000 deaths in an office, or workplace, every single day. Equally as staggering: worldwide, there are 340 million workplace accidents and 160 million victims of work-related illnesses annually. These figures, from the International Labour Organization, are only increasing in number year on year. Think twice, before you decide to go into work today.

#1 Playlist
How To Make It
Through Monday

Hung-over? Tired? Skint? Anxiety-riddled? Yep, that sounds like
Monday. This playlist will help ease you in to the working week...

▶ 1. **Mo Money Mo Problems – The Notorious B.I.G.**

▶ 2. **Opportunities (Let's Make Lots of Money) –
       Pet Shop Boys**

▶ 3. **Don't Talk To Me About Work – Lou Reed**

▶ 4. **Seven Days of the Week (I Never Go To Work) –
       They Might Be Giants**

▶ 5. **I Don't Like Mondays – The Boomtown Rats**

▶ 6. **Working Class Hero – John Lennon**

▶ 7. **Slave to the Grind – Skid Row**

▶ 8. **Just Another Manic Monday – The Bangles**

▶ 9. **Hard Knock Life – Jay Z**

▶ 10. **A Hard Day's Night – The Beatles**

Office History #1: The Office Chair

Don't waste time clock-watching while sat at your desk. That's boring. Instead, waste time reading the paragraph below. It's both boring and fascinating at the same time.

The one thing you'll spend the rest of your life sitting on – the humble office chair – was actually invented by Charles Darwin, in the 1800s. Yes, *that* Charles Darwin. For those of you who went to school, he needs no introduction. For the rest (majority?) of you, Charles Darwin was the man who changed the world by theorizing, correctly as it turned out, that all life has evolved from previous species. He also invented the office chair. Amazingly, Darwin was the first bright spark to add wheels to the legs of his laboratory chair – so, we assume, he could zoom around to observe his exotic platypus specimens more quickly.

Like I said, boring *and* fascinating.

People In The Office You Love To Hate

Chances are you won't be one of them, so who exactly are the ten coolest people where you work?

1

The Person Who Always Has A More Fun Weekend Than You

"On Saturday I got a last-minute flight and went Great White Shark diving in South Africa… and then on Sunday I joyrode a car into a newsagent's!"

2

The Person Who Always Uses Sexual Innuendo

"The postman's just delivered a massive package for me."

3

The Person Who Always Brings In Cake

"It's the day after Monday, so I thought you all deserved some cake."

4

The Person Who Knows Everything

"Yeah, of course I saw the report. I see everything before anyone. But I want to know what you thought of it?"

5

The Person Who Is Always Pregnant

"I just like how being pregnant *feels*, you know? Plus, I get to leave early."

Secrets Of Success

Most bosses these days will tell you that they've never looked at your Facebook page. That is a lie. A wicked lie. To circumvent having to lie to your boss about what you did at the weekend – where there are ample amounts of evidence to suggest you were anything but the clean-cut, sober, kiss-ass persona you have worked hard to install as your default personality – simply create *two* Facebook accounts. Tell your co-workers about the boring one and keep the other one a secret. Post cat pictures to one, drunken naked selfies to the other. Never the twain shall meet.

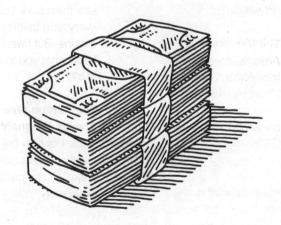

Things To Doodle During Meetings

We all know meetings are the most unproductive part of the working week. Nothing is ever achieved, time is only wasted. And yet they have become a crucial part of office life. Why not waste more time with these top ten meeting notes that will have your co-workers stifling awkward laughs:

1   **Self-portrait** – doodle a picture of yourself as how you think you look in the meeting. Don't forget to add dead-looking eyes and a stifled yawn.

2   **A sketch of your boss** – an intricate line drawing of your boss, or whoever is "leading" the meeting. Make sure you include stink lines and speech bubbles filled with the words "BLAH BLAH BLAH".

3   **Join the dots** – sketch out a vivid and intricate scene of workplace death and destruction, perhaps even a murder of a work colleague, in glorious join-the-dots format, so no one knows what you're up to!

4   **Reinterpret a work of art** – reimagine the Mona Lisa, or Banksy's Heart Balloon girl, but draw your co-workers' faces on them, instead of the masterpieces.

5   **Inspirational quotes** – These should already be writ large on your notepad. Alternatively, scribble on top of the meeting agenda the motivational words of whomever you can think of.

6   Write the words **"YOU DON'T HAVE TO BE MAD TO WORK HERE BUT IT HELPS!"** in large child-like type all over your meeting notes.

7 If your notepad is lined, spend the entire meeting writing the same repetitive line over and over again. This is a good one:

I must pay attention in meetings, I must pay attention in meetings

8 **Create a monster** – doodle a creature as fierce and as devilish as you see in your mind's eye. Perhaps the monster has the face of your boss. Maybe add some spice by have the monster devouring a caricature of one of your co-workers. Don't forget to name it, too!

9 **Design a flipbook** – a personal favourite. Use the fact that most meetings go on for hours longer than first specified, and use that extra time wisely. With your notepad, create a Flip Book so awesome that even after the meeting finishes, you'll still be engrossed after everyone else has left the room. Good scenes that work for Flip Books are: sharks eating a surfer, spear-throwing, a man getting their tie caught in a shredder and your boss's head exploding into a thousand tiny pieces.

10 **A Penis** – with hairy balls and ejaculation lines for good measure. Perhaps name it "El Grande", for flavour.

Office Dares #2: Emojis

Emojis are everywhere these days, people are getting sick of them. Next time you want to pull a sickie, why not use an emoji to tell your boss you're not feeling very well. Like so…

-----------Original Message-------------
From: jsmith@workworkwork.com
Sent: Thursday, 11 June 2015, 09.15am
Subject: Feeling unwell

Dear [*insert name of boss*],

I am feeling 😵 and 👎
I'll head to the if I don't feel any better.
I wont come to the office for fear of 🤢
Will stay at 🏠
Thanks,
😷🖕

Top Ten: Fonts To Glamourize Dull Work Emails

If you really want to piss off your co-workers – and you really should want to – then these are the greatest fonts to use in serious communications to really achieve that objective. They add a little spice to the otherwise meaningless corporate jargon you have to send. Best used at point size 18.

1 Curlz MT

2 BLACKOAK STD

3 MARKER FELT

4 Edwardian Script ITC

5 DESDEMONA

6 ROSEWOOD STD

7 ZAPFINO

8 Handwriting – Dakota

9 Lucida Handwriting

10 BRAGGADOCIO

REMEMBER:
Nothing says, "I'm completely serious about the work I do" than… using **COMIC SANS MS** in *all* your work emails. Try it out. You'll be fired by the end of the day.

Top 5:
Out Of Office Messages

Out of Office messages are so dull. Wouldn't it be great if we could jazz them up a little...with the truth!

-----------Original Message-------------
From: jsmith@workworkwork.com
Sent: Wednesday, 24 December 2015, 09.00am
Subject: Christmas Eve

My body may physically present in the office today, but my mind, soul and spirit, is already out the door… and has been since 01 December.

Your email will now not be read until January 03.

If your query is urgent…tough sh*t. You should have sent it to me sooner.

Happy Holidays.

-----------Original Message-------------
From: jsmith@workworkwork.com
Sent: Friday, 16 January 2015, 3:05pm
Subject: Out Of Office

I am currently out of the office.

If you wish for your email to be placed at the top of my inbox for when I return, please press your thumb on the hyperlink below. CLICK HERE*

*Clicks through to www.Hotbottoms.co.uk

-----------Original Message-------------
From: jsmith@workworkwork.com
Sent: Friday, 16 January 2015, 3:05pm
Subject: Out Of Office

Hi, I'm Troy McClure. You might remember me from such previous Out of Office Messages as I've Gone to a Dentist's Appointment that Definitely Exists And Is Not A Job interview, and I'm Not Feeling Very Well...But It Has Nothing To Do With Getting Drunk Last Night.

-----------Original Message-------------
From: jsmith@workworkwork.com
Sent: Friday, 16 January 2015, 3:05pm
Subject: Out Of Office

I am out of the office until 17/11/16. I will be unable to delete all the emails you send me until I return from my well-deserved holiday away from you idiots. Rest assured your email will be deleted in the order it was received.

Thanks.

-----------Original Message-------------
From: jsmith@workworkwork.com
Sent: Tuesday, 11 June 2015, 17.29pm
Subject: Holiday Handover

I am now on holiday for two weeks. I will not be reading my emails while I am away.

I also "forgot" to do a handover holiday form. I sort of got the feeling that none of you cared about my work.

Have fun talking about me while I'm away. Thanks.

#2 Playlist
Thank Goodness
It's Friday

It's the last day of the working week. You deserve to blow off some steam with these killer jams laser-focused to put you into a good mood.

▶ 1. **Pharrell Williams – Happy**

▶ 2. **Bill Withers – Lovely Day**

▶ 3. **U2 – Beautiful Day**

▶ 4. **Katrina & The Waves – Walking On Sunshine**

▶ 5. **Ed Sheeran – Sing**

▶ 6. **Wham! – Wake Me Up Before You Go-Go**

▶ 7. **Avicii – Wake Me Up**

▶ 8. **The Killers – Mr. Brightside**

▶ 9. **Cat Stevens – Morning Has Broken**

▶ 10. **Katy Perry – Roar**

Email Nation

In the time it took you to read this sentence, 20 million emails were sent around the world. You – yes, YOU! – spend on average 11.2 hours a week reading and replying to emails, which accounts for wasting 28 per cent of your 40-hour working week.

www.factsaboutwww.com

If it weren't for the world wide web, our jobs would be 87 per cent more crap and boring than they already are. We owe, quite literally, our whole lives to this handy little invention that makes our lives so much easier. But how much do we really know about it? Here are some interesting facts to rely on next time you are stuck in the lift having awkward conversations with the IT manager.

1 Ray Tomlinson sent the first email to himself in 1971. "The test messages were entirely forgettable... Most likely the first message was QWERTYIOP or something similar," he said.

2 The first domain name ever registered was Symbolics. com on March 15, 1985. Now it serves as a historic site.

3 The first website was dedicated to information about the World Wide Web and went live on August 6, 1991. Here's the URL: http://info.cern.ch/hypertext/WWW/ TheProject.html.

4 The first book purchased on Amazon was Douglas Hofstadter's *Fluid Concepts and Creative Analogies: Computer Models of the Fundamental Mechanisms of Thought* in 1995.

5 Mark Zuckerberg was the first person to be added as a friend on Facebook with ID number 4 (the first three Facebook accounts ever created were used for testing).

Anti-Social Media

We spend a lot of working day wasting time on social media, chatting and communicating with other people, who are often many miles away. While it's not surprising to know that we would much rather converse with our friends in other offices than the people sitting next to us in our own, a recent survey concluded that, across all age groups, office workers spend an average of 42.1 minutes per day on Facebook, with 18–29-year-olds dedicating 51 minutes of their office hours to it; this represents about 28 per cent of all daily online activity. More than 1.1 billion active Facebook users upload 350 million photos daily, 30 per cent of which are food, and another 30 per cent are selfies.

Lost In Translation

Offices may be full of foreign-speaking internationals fluent in a multitude of exotic languages, but office small talk is still dull, boring and petty, no matter how hard you dress it up. But it doesn't have to be. Make your office small talk more exciting today by impressing your international colleagues with your knowledge of dull and boring office objects in other languages. Don't just ask your Dutch co-worker for a stapler, for example – demand a "Nietmachine"!

Stapler	**Nietmachine**	Dutch
	Grapagailua	Basque
	Heftalica	Bosnian
	Grapadora	Catalan
	Agrafeuse	French
	Hefter	German
	Spillatrice	Italian
	Zszywacz	Polish

Photocopier	**Fotocopiadora**	Spanish
	Fotokopjuese	Albanian
	Fotokopieerapparaat	Dutch
	Valokopiokone	Finnish
	Fotokopiergerät	German
	Kopiarka	Polish
	fotokopi makinesi	Turkish

Phone	**Telefoon**	Dutch
	Telephonon	Esperanto
	Puhelin	Finnish
	Siminn	Icelandic
	Xov tooj	Hmong
	Foonu	Yoruba
	Simu	Swahili

Fire Alarm	**Alarm zjarri**	Albanian
	Sunog	Cebuano

	protivpožarni alarm	Bosnian
	umlilo alamu	Zulu
	požární hlásič	Czech
	alarma de incendio	Galician
	yangın heyecanı	Azerbajiani
	fajro alarmo	Esperanto
	alarem kahuruan	Sundanese
	brandalarm	Danish
	ugunsgrēka trauksme	Latvian

Computer	Ordinador	Catalan
	Kompjuter	Bosnian
	Tietokone	Finnish
	Tölva	Icelandic
	Počítač	Slovak
	Calculator	Romanian
	ordinateur	French
	računalo	Croatian

Meeting	Takim	Albanian
	sastanak	Bosnian
	vergadering	Dutch
	kohtumine	Estonian
	reunion	French
	Sitzung	German
	Fundi	Icelandic
	Behlangana	Zulu

Bored	Gelangweilt	German
	Znuděný	Czech
	Ennuyé	French
	Kyllästynyt	Finnish
	Unott	Hungarian
	Leiðindi	Icelandic
	Leamh	Irish
	Bıkkın	Turkish
	Uttråkad	Swedish

Quote Quota #19

**" Be nice to nerds.
Chances are you'll end up
working for one. "**

Bill Gates

Speaking In Code

A brilliant way to waste time at work is to devise a code system
with a mate or your partner, where work-related words and phrases
can be substituted for non-working words. By doing this, you can
make a "personal call" sound a lot like a "work call". Here are some
beginner code words to get you started:

WORD	CODEWORD
Working hard	How are you doing?
Busy right now	How was your evening last night?
Completing objectives	Bored of Facebook for today
Meeting targets	What are you doing this weekend?
Working late	Fancy meeting at 5.30 sharp for a beer?
Global economic crisis	I'm getting really drunk tonight
Deadline looming	I'm not doing any work today
Client facing	What are you wearing?
Hungry for results	What are we having for dinner?
Goal orientated	Is there football on tonight?
Require extra incentives	I'll nick some toilet paper from the office toilet

Obviously, if you want longer conversations, you'll have to devise
more code. But once you become fluent in the code, you'll be
spending your whole day chatting "work" to your mate or partner
without arousing suspicion. Alternatively, if this all just seems too
much like hard work, then feel free to just make personal phone calls
from your desk and see if anyone actually notices. Chances are,
nobody gives a damn.

Office Poetry

Ten minutes spent on the Internet doing research and look what happens – we find this doozy of a poem about life in an office from more than two hundred years ago. Take that, libaries!

From ten to eleven, have breakfast for seven;

From eleven to noon, think you've come too soon;

From twelve to one, think what's to be done;

From one to two, find nothing to do;

From two to three, think it will be

A very great bore to stay till four.

Thomas Love Peacock
(who spent his working life at the East India Company – the world's first recognized office – in the 1790s)

When Words Fail, Part 1

Sometimes in offices words can fail to explain exactly how we feel. In these occasions we must turn to other languages to find *le mot juste*. The words below have no direct English equivalent but can be perfectly experienced in every office all over the globe:

1 **Kummerspeck (German)**
The excess weight gained from overeating due to stress from work. Literally, means "grief bacon". I think we can all relate to that.

2 **Shemomedjamo (Georgian)**
When you've eaten so much at lunchtime that you literally couldn't eat another bite. This word means, "I accidentally ate the whole thing."

3 **Tartle (Scots)**
This is the panicky hesitation you feel just before you have to introduce someone whose name you can't quite remember. Happens all the time in work situations when introducing the New Guy.

4 **Backpfeifengesicht (German)**
The perfect word to describe all middle management types – "A face badly in need of a fist." As so often, the Germans nail it.

5 **Iktsuarpok (Inuit)**
This word describes that feeling of anticipation when you're waiting for someone to show up at your workplace and you keep going to the reception see if they're there yet.

Office History #2:
The Ballpoint Pen

The Ballpoint Pen – the one item that no office can function without even in these days of word processors, laptops and keyboards. Ballpoint Pens are still a crucial part of our everyday office life, even if they are now predominantly used for chewing, doodling hairy penises in meetings and writing "HATE YOUR JOB? CALL BEEFY ON 0900654376 FOR GUARANTEED RELIEF" on the office toilet door. Before the Ballpoint Pen became the weapon of choice in offices all around the world for the last 75 years, it was just a figment of one man's imagination…

Before the onset of the Second World War in 1939, a Jewish-Hungarian journalist by the name of László Bíró was getting fed up of fountain-pen ink spotting and splashing his papers, ruining them in the process. So, after one day of visiting a Budapest printing shop, he observed a type of quick-drying ink used in printing and wondered if it could replace the liquid ink used in fountain pens? Bíró, and his brother George, set to work, and after several years of experiments, they replaced their prototype metal writing nib with a tiny ball bearing in its tip, and relied on capillary action (the very same process used by leaves to suck water up in plants). Now, when the pen scribbled along the paper, the ball rolled, picking up ink from the attached tube of ink and setting it down evenly on the surface of paper. No blobs, no blots, no stains. Job done.

Today, the rolling ball in a Ballpoint Pen still takes up to 60 hours to make, and is less than a millimetre wide. It is as hard as a diamond, and yet you'll lose (and possibly swallow) 50 of them every single year without even caring.

Bic, the leading manufacturer of Bíró's Biro, has sold more than 215 million pens in Britain alone. Since 1950, Baron Marcel Bich (now Bic), the savvy entrepreneur who bought the patent off Bíró, has sold more than 100 billion ballpoint pens globally. That's enough ink to draw a line to the moon and back more than 320,000 times!

People In The Office You Love To Hate

Know-it-alls, smug buggers, ego-maniacs, and kiss-asses – they may look just like you and me, but don't be fooled, they are here solely to rumble your goat between 9 and 5. Here are a few of the real villains you'll "touch base" with today.

The Person Who Always Makes the Tea
"Sorry I'm so late for this meeting… but I was just making you all tea. I really hope I didn't miss anything?"

The Person Who Doesn't Care About Anything
"Did I do the thing you asked me to do? Nah – couldn't see the point."

The Person Who Always Leaves On Time
"They pay me until 5.30. At 5.29 I'm putting my coat on..."

The IT Manager
"Nobody has a clue what I do. I just watch YouTube all day and buy stuff on eBay. When I'm really bored I look on the Dark Web."

The Person Who Makes Plans Every Night Of The Week
"Yeah, tonight I'm seeing a play, tomorrow a charity event, then a football match, then a swinger's party and then a mass protest. Probably, just chill at the weekend."

When Words Fail, Part 2

The words below have no direct English equivalent but can be perfectly experienced in every office all over the globe:

1 **Greng-jai (Thai)**
This word explains that awkward moment when you don't want someone else to do something for you because it would be a pain for them, even though you really want them to. For example, "It's OK, I'll spend hours writing up the minutes to that boring meeting… I know *you* have better things to do."

2 **Gigil (Filipino)**
The curse of the office: the urge to pinch or squeeze something that is irresistibly cute, usually an attractive colleague's bottom.

3 **Zeg (Georgian)**
If you could get away with saying "Zeg" in meetings, it would save you the embarrassment of having to say you'll get the job done "the day after tomorrow" and not today, as promised.

4 **Boketto (Japanese)**
The act of gazing vacantly into the distance. A common aspect of every office worker's job description.

5 **L'esprit de l'escalier (French)**
Literally, "stairwell wit" – a too-late retort thought usually only after everybody has left the room. Most meetings conclude with this feeling.

Playlist Songs To Play Really Loud To Annoy Your Boss

Managers – you know who you are. You know we don't like you… and these are the perfect songs to make sure you get the message loud and clear.

- ▶ 1. **Won't Get Fooled Again – The Who**
- ▶ 2. **You and Whose Army? – Radiohead**
- ▶ 3. **My Way – Sid Vicious**
- ▶ 4. **Working For The Man – PJ Harvey**
- ▶ 5. **Another Brick in the Wall – Pink Floyd**
- ▶ 6. **Big Boss Man – Grateful Dead**
- ▶ 7. **Boss of Me – David Bowie**
- ▶ 8. **Boss Life – Snoop Dogg**
- ▶ 9. **Always Your Way – My Vitriol**
- ▶ 10. **Like a Boss – The Lonely Island**
- ▶ 11. **Battle of Who Could Care Less – Ben Folds Five**
- ▶ 12. **Bye Bye Bad Man – Stone Roses**
- ▶ 13. **Don't Make Me A Target – Spoon**
- ▶ 14. **Everything You Didn't Do – Jamie Cullum**
- ▶ 15. **Get Me Away From Here, I'm Dying – Belle and Sebastian**
- ▶ 16. **Go To Hell – David Ford**
- ▶ 17. **How To Disappear Completely – Radiohead**
- ▶ 18. **I Am Not A Robot – Marina and The Diamonds**
- ▶ 19. **I'm Looking Through You – The Beatles**
- ▶ 20. **Lost Worker Bee – Elbow**

iRobot

About 35 per cent of all office roles in the UK are at high risk of computerization and automation over the next two decades, according to a study by researchers at Oxford University and Deloitte. This gives all us office drones something to celebrate!

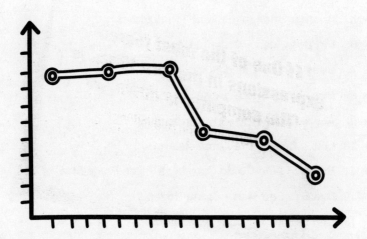

Quote Quota #42

❝ One of the most feared expressions in modern times is 'The computer is down.' ❞

Norman Ralph Augustine

Top Ten Office Hates

There are many reasons why co-workers bicker and fight with each other: the kind of food we eat, how loud we talk on the phone, whether we stink of cigarettes or how much we kiss our boss's asses. While 44 per cent of people admitted to confronting their co-workers' bad habits, the rest of us appear to just accept that it's not part of the job.

WOMEN'S TOP TEN OFFICE HATES

1 Eating smelly food

2 Being late

3 Too many cigarette breaks

4 Bad hygiene

5 Not being organized

6 Messy desk

7 Colleagues not returning borrowed stationery

8 Talking on the phone too loudly

9 Taking too long for lunch

10 Dressing inappropriately

MEN'S TOP TEN OFFICE HATES

1 Messy desk

2 Colleagues spraying perfume or aftershave

3 Talking on the phone too loud

4 Being late

5 Taking too long for lunch

6 Eating smelly food

7 Too many cigarette breaks

8 Colleagues talking too much

9 Not being organized

10 Rudeness

Corporate Bollocks

This is wanky corporate jargon at its best. How many of these dreadful phrases have you said today?

BOLLOCKS	UNDERSTANDABLE
Going Forward	Progress
Idea Showers	Thinking
Incentivize	Blackmail / Manipulate
Product Evangelist	Believes in the product
Platform Atheist	Doesn't believe in the product
Touch Base	Communicate
Loop Back	Speak later
Low Hanging Fruit	Achievable Goal
360-degree thinking	Thinking
Close of Play	End of the Day
110 per cent	100 per cent (Quite a lot!)
Wrongside	Second guess

Quote Quota #5

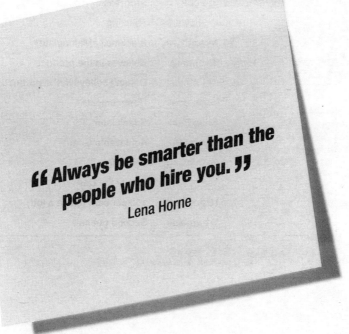

" Always be smarter than the people who hire you. "
Lena Horne

Mandatory Fun

Working isn't all bad. Here are the ten best things about going to work in an office, as polled from a recent survey:

1

2

3

4

5

6

7

8

9

10 Leaving work to go home.

Office History #3:
The Paperclip

The humble paper clip has a mysterious origin. No one knows for sure when the first paper clip was invented, by whom, and where – some say Norway, some Germany, some say America. But what we do know is that the modern paper clip – the thing you'll use to poke the breakfast burrito out from in-between your teeth – is that three trillion have been produced since 1899, with American workplaces consuming 11 billion every year alone – that's around 10,000 for every person in the United States for each year! The name of the most common type of paperclip found in an office is called the Gem, presumed to have been invented around the 1880–90s.

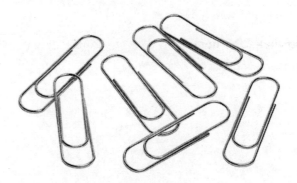

Office Dares #5: SFW – Safe For Work

Tease your IT Manager, or whoever it is whose job is to scour through the web history of every employee to check for pornography or other "non work-related and inappropriate" websites, and check out these websites below. They are all SFW (Safe For Work), despite what their name suggests....

1. **Whorepresents.com** (Who Represents)
2. **Penisland.net** (Pen Island)
3. **Expertsexchange.com** (Experts Exchange)
4. **Speedofart.com** (Speed of Art)
5. **Lesbocages.com** (Les Bocages)
6. **Therapistfinder.com** (Therapist Finder)
7. **Dicksonweb.com** (Dickson Web)
8. **Powergenitalia.com** (Powergen Italia)
9. **Teacherstalking.org** (Teachers Talking)
10. **Childrenswear.co.uk** (Childrens Wear)

Office History #4:
The Photocopier

Who cares?

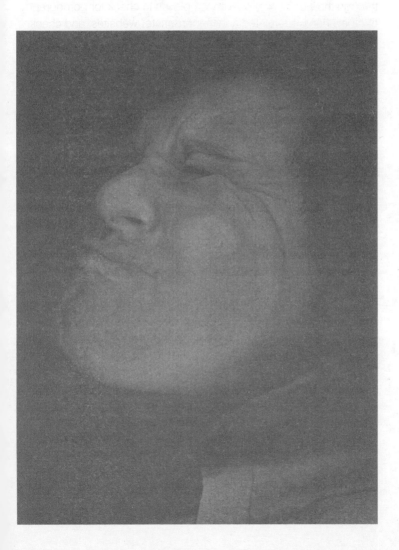

How To Make The Perfect Paper Aeroplane

A decade ago, with the advent of the Internet, emails and hard drives, we all thought that by the year 2015, we'd be commuting to work on our hoverboards and working in "paperless offices". Alas, neither of those things has come true. We still waste as much pristine, pure-as snow, gleaming white 100gsm A4 paper as we have ever used. While most of us are spectacularly environment-conscious, there are a few dinosaurs in the office who still print documents out like there is no tomorrow, simply because they find it easier to read than on the screen.

To counterbalance these morons, let's put their waste to good use. Any time you see printed pieces of A4 paper going to waste, don't just put it straight in the recycling bin. It is your environmental duty to have a bit of fun with it first.

Here's how:

Here are our easy step-by-step instructions. For hilarious results, use paper that has swear words printed all over one side.

 Non-sweary side up. Fold the page in half along Line 1.

 **Open the paper up again. Fold down corners towards you so that they meet at the centre fold.**

3 Now fold the triangle made by A & B down the non-sweary side.

4 Take corners C and D and fold them in towards the centre of the page until their points touch E and F respectively.

5 This is what you should have so far– the sweary side is now showing.

6 Now fold up the little triangle marked "FLAP" so that it covers (and "locks") corners C & D.

7 Fold the paper back in half along down the centre line.

8 Now fold down the "wings" along so that the two halves of the plane meet.

Run Of The Mill

A single tree, a softwood tree such as a spruce, fir, larch or hemlock, accounts for 7,560 pieces of A4 paper. A moden office of 50 staff uses, on average, 300 pieces of paper a day. One office uses an entire tree worth of paper every 15 days (give or take). And for what? Meeting minutes? Telephone Lists? What a waste. It takes a poor spruce tree 20 years to grow to maturity. This book alone will waste at least 100 trees worth of paper.

Sick Of Work

A 2015 study has found that within 2–4 hours of a sick person touching an office doorknob, table top or common surface, 40–60% of their coworkers become infected.

If you want to cause maximum disruption to the office – and spread your dreaded lurgy everywhere – then the best thing to do is organize a meeting pronto. Now everyone will be ill. Goal!

Quote Quota #77

> **❝ Eight hours work, eight hours sleep, eight hours play, make a just and healthy day. ❞**
> King Alfred the Great

Office Dare #6 – Email Roulette

Open up a new email. Type in a swear word of your choice in the Subject Line. Click in the "Send To" line. Close your eyes. Type in any letter on the keyboard. Whoever's name pops up, send the email to them. No chickening out allowed.

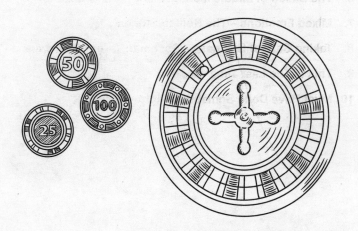

Playlist – Post Appraisal Soundtrack

Do you sometimes wonder whose side your boss is on?

- ▶ 1. **Which Side Are You On? – Pete Seeger**
- ▶ 2. **Take This Job and Shove It – Johnny Paycheck**
- ▶ 3. **Feel Like A Number – Bob Seger**
- ▶ 4. **Shaddup You Face – Joe Dolce**
- ▶ 5. **I Can't Wait To Get Off Work – Tom Waits**
- ▶ 6. **The Ballad of Middle Management – The Breakers**
- ▶ 7. **Mixed Emotions – The Rolling Stones**
- ▶ 8. **Taking Care of Business – Bachman Turner Overdrive**
- ▶ 9. **This Is The Last Time – Keane**
- ▶ 10. **Must Have Done Something Right – Relient K**

Office Dare – Create An Alternative Company History On The Firm's Wikipedia Page

If you work for a big multinational corporation, or even just a successful start-up or a micro company, most businesses these days have a Wikipedia page. The best way to look like your boning up your company's history, while actually sticking it to the Man, is to edit your company's Wikipedia page instead, adding choice funny words, gibberish and lies.

There's No "I" In Team Meetings

The epitome of boredom, team meetings are full of saying and doing the same thing week in, week out, but never actually achieving anything. There is always room for improvement; try these certified techniques of inserting mindlessness into your daily meetings:

1. **Stare off into the middle distance, disengage with all conversation.**
2. **Yawn loudly whenever your boss begins to talk.**
3. **Stand up and shout "Yes!" when the meeting is finally over.**
4. **Draw genitalia on your notepad, and then point them out proudly to colleagues.**

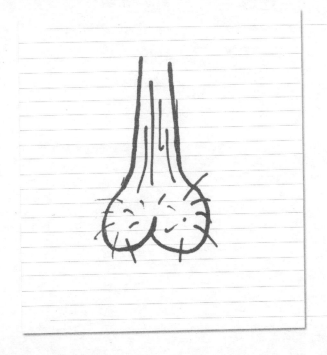

Quote Quota #21

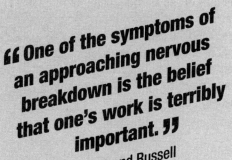

❝ One of the symptoms of an approaching nervous breakdown is the belief that one's work is terribly important. ❞
Bertrand Russell

An Office Joke For IT Geeks

You don't have to be a robot to work here… but 10101010000011100101.

Tie Fighters

Hundreds of millions of ties are bought to accessorize the pale and lifeless office uniform every single year. These corporate nooses are, quite literally, garotting the life out of us every single day. Hilariously, it is believed that at one point in history merely touching a man's tie knot was cause for a duel. That's how important ties were considered. These days, two men touching each other's ties in the workplace is usually cause for a duet.

Guidelines For Working From Home

Working from home is your God-given employee's duty at least once a month. Duvet Days are becoming popular, but nothing says "I simply can't be bothered to work today" better than calling your boss from your bed and telling them you are "working from home". Here's how to do it right.

1 Pyjamas are compulsory all day

2 Stay in bed until the moment you start feeling guilty about still being in bed

3 Order a pizza for delivery – saves leaving the house

4 Down tools at 5.30 like you would if you'd gone to work – and even if you have achieved nothing

5 Have daytime TV always on in the background

6 Chat to the elderly neighbour, in case you require someone to talk to

7 Phone your parents and tell them how busy work is at the moment

8 Go to the local shop at lunch and buy a treat – because you're worth it

9 Have a long bath, so that you can say you at least washed yourself today

10 Call your friends in the office and tell them what you are watching on TV

Quote Quota #56

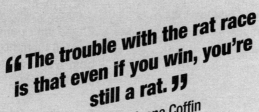

❝ The trouble with the rat race is that even if you win, you're still a rat. ❞

William Sloane Coffin

Terms And Conditions Apply

Thirty-five per cent of the world's workforce loathes their job. If you've had enough of working long hours for little pay and no reward, then fill out an application form for the world's easiest jobs today:

1. **Lifeguard** (no-one hardly ever needs saving, let's be honest)

2. **Sports mascot** (working in fancy dress – what's not to love?)

3. **Living statue** (you literally get paid to do nothing)

4. **Ice cream man** (scoop ice cream into a cone, drive around and repeat. Job done)

5. **Cat sitter** (sit with a cat, get paid, go home)

6. **Buckingham Palace Guard** (your only job requirement is to stand there and do nothing.)

Office Dares #8 – Make A Voodoo Doll Of Your Boss

A great way to waste ten minutes of your day is to collect as much Blu-Tack as possible from around the office and to sculpt it into a Voodoo Doll that bares a great resemblance to your manager, or a co-worker you despise. A great way to ensure a strong sense of likeness is to buy a *Star Wars* toy figure (1:6 ratio) – Han Solo is the best if your boss is a man, Princess Leia if she is female – and cover the toy in Blu-Tack until it resembles a blue human figure. Now you are free to dress and decorate the figure to match your enemy, but the sharp notice board pins you use stay in nice and firmly when you poke the doll repeatedly in the groin.

Dance Moves To Avoid At Office Parties

When we're sober, we are all too shy to bust out our A-game dance moves, but after a few gin and tonics, all of a sudden these dance moves get dusted off in order to impress our equally intoxicated colleagues. AVOID THESE MOVES AT ALL COSTS THOUGH... they'll be the talk of the office the next day:

1. **The Moon Walk**
2. **The Van Halen "Jump"**
3. **The MC Hammer**
4. **The Twerk – RESIST ALL TEMPTATION!**
5. **The Sprinkler**
6. **The Robot – RESIST ALL TEMPTATION!**
7. **The Power Knee Slide**
8. **The Worm**
9. **The Grind**
10. **Beyoncé's "Single Ladies" routine**

Office Anagram

An anagram of "office" may well be the fancy French hair-related word, coiffe (as well as almost, if you squint, "coffee"), but why not waste the rest of the afternoon figuring out the cool anagrams to these work-related words?

1. **Snooze Alarms – Alas No More Zs**

2. **A Decimal Point – I'm A Dot In Place**

3. **Desperation – A Rope Ends It**

4. **Conversation – Voices Rant On**

5. **Microsoft Windows – Sown in discomfort**

6. **Listen – Silent**

7. **Software – I swear oft**

8. **Christmas – Trims cash**

Playlist – Songs To Motivate You

It's nearly 5.00pm and you've still got tons of work to do. This playlist will help you make sure you leave on time….

▸ 1. **Taylor Swift – Shake It Off**

▸ 2. **Coldplay – Viva La Vida**

▸ 3. **Michael Jackson – Don't Stop 'Til You Get Enough**

▸ 4. **Aretha Franklin – Respect**

▸ 5. **Lady Gaga – Poker Face**

▸ 6. **The Killers – Human**

▸ 7. **AC/DC – Thunderstruck**

▸ 8. **No Doubt – Don't Speak**

▸ 9. **The White Stripes – Seven Nation Army**

▸ 10. **George Ezra – Blame it on Me**

Office Kitchen Commandments

Despite the dozens of signs that officious rule-followers put up all over the kitchen walls, please make sure you NEVER follow their incessant and irritating instructions:

1. **Please clean up after yourself**

2. **Please put away items after use**

3. **Please clean up any spillages**

4. **Please throw away any smelly/rotting food**

5. **Please close the refrigerator door**

6. **Please label your items and store in proper containers**

7. **Please only eat foodstuffs that you provide**

8. **Please only use coffee and mugs that have not been designated by others**

9. **Never de-limescale the kettle without telling anyone**

10.**If you break a mug, please replace it.**

Office Dares #111 – Mug Fun

After someone sends out an all-staff email asking "if anyone has seen my mug...", go on a mission around the office to help find the mug. Once located, hide it. Hide it in a place where it will never be found. Then laugh maniacally to yourself, like this: "Muah, hah, hah, hah, hah, muah, hah, hah, muah, hah, hah," and so on...

Office Toilet Commandments

These are the only rules of the office that you are never allowed to bend or break…

1 Never poo in a urinal

2 Never wee in the sink

3 Never write graffiti on the toilet door (people will recognize your handwriting)

4 Always refill the toilet roll if it runs out on your watch

5 Always scrub the porcelain – no brown streaks or stains allowed

6 Never leave wee on the seat

7 Never talk about work while standing at a urinal next to a colleague

8 Never make small chat with the person sat in the cubicle next to yours

9 Never spend more than ten minutes sitting down

10 Always open the window

Golden Rule: If you can smell your own, it's ten times worse for everyone else.

The Office Bad Boy / Girl

You can spot them a mile off – usually doing all of the following:

1 Strolls in 30-minutes late every day, smelling of lager perfume

2 Wears the same clothes three days in a row

3 Confidently walks out the office early, doesn't care who sees

4 Talks on his phone loudly about "what a mess" he was the night before

5 Has friends called Eggsy, Oggy and Laddsy

6 Never replies to emails that aren't directly addressed to him

7 Says "That's what she said" after all possible opportunities for innuendo

8 Disappears for hours at a time at out of office "meetings"

9 Organizes after work drinks, but then never goes

10 Tweets hourly about how bored he is at work

Anti-Work Rules, Part 1

Every office has rules, or guidelines, for appropriate behaviour and etiquette. Ignore them. Follow these instead:

1 Never walk without a folder or bunch of documents in your hands

2 Always leave the office at home-time carrying a load of documents in two hands

3 Never walk round carrying a newspaper – it looks like you're off to the toilet for a few hours

4 Never walk out of the office with your smartphone at your ear while saying the words, "Hold on a minute, mate" – it looks as if someone is calling you to buy drugs

5 Use your computer to look busy – open up a Word document full of text, and flit back to that screen when somebody walks past. It'll save you having to explain why the only thing people see open on your desktop is Safari or Internet Explorer

6 Make sure your desk looks messy. A clean desk is an unbusy mind. It's volume that counts, so pile your paper up as high as possible

Quote Quota #34

" Any organization is like a septic tank. The big chunks rise to the top. "

John Imhoff

Office Dare 11 – Photoshop Tennis

The rules of this dare are easy. First select your group. Then all start by opening up an image editing software programme, such as Photoshop or Paint. The first person, picked at random, starts off by drawing an illustration of the Boss – but only completes the head, for example. The first person then emails that Photoshop file over to the second person, who draws another body part, then sends that file over to another person, and so on until every member of the group has added to it. The final person of the group has to finish of the drawing, title it, then print it off and stick to the Boss's office door, or somewhere public. Because it's all done in Photoshop – and the work of several people – the Boss will have no idea who did it! It's the perfect crime and displays not only disloyalty to your shared enemy but also the ability of you and your colleagues to work perfectly as a team.

Think Outside
The Box

Look at the box below. But not inside in. Look on the outside of the box. Concentrate all of your thoughts there. What do you see?

Don't look here! **Look here!**

First Jobs Of The Rich And Famous: Top 10 – Part 1

No matter whether you're Brad Pitt or Jimmy Osmond, Justin Bieber or just a beaver, all of us on Planet Earth have to start somewhere. And that somewhere is usually pretty dreadful. Thankfully celebrities aren't immune to our struggles, with many of the world's most glamorous people having started their careers on their knees covered in dirt. It's a dirty job, but someone's got to do it…

1. **Kurt Cobain – Janitor**

2. **David Bowie – Butcher's delivery boy**

3. **Ozzy Osbourne – Abattoir worker ("I had to slice open the cow carcasses and get the entire gunk out of their stomachs. I used to vomit every day.")**

4. **Mick Jagger – Hospital porter**

5. **Freddie Mercury – Market stall owner**

6. **Jarvis Cocker – Fishmonger**

7. **Jay Z – Drug dealer**

8. **Rod Stewart – Gravedigger**

9. **Morrissey – inland Revenue worker**

10. **Jack White – Upholsterer**

This Way Up

You've got 45 minutes before lunchtime. Why not kill the time, and match the celebrities below to their height. I admit it's not fun, but it's no doubt ten times more fun than any work you have to do.

1. **Taylor Swift**
2. **Prince**
3. **Robert Downey Jr.**
4. **Kim Kardashian**
5. **Kate Middleton**
6. **Miley Cyrus**
7. **Kanye West**
8. **Ryan Gosling**

a) **5'9½"**
b) **5'2"**
c) **5'9"**
d) **5'3"**
e) **5'10"**
f) **5'5"**
g) **5'8"**
h) **6'0"**

(If you really need the answers – Google them.)

Anti Work Rules, Part 2

Working hard doesn't have to be tough. If you're smart, you can work hard by hardly working. Here's how:

1 Never answer your phone. Always let it go to voicemail. If it's important, they'll leave a message. People call only because they want you to do their work for them. People never call to take work away from you, do they?

2 Don't just look busy – look upset and stressed and physically get angry when you receive an email, as if you're a martyr to your work. This gives the impression that you care. Ha!

3 Set up your email account on your smartphone to schedule sending work emails you wrote during the working day, at 06:00 and 9:30 at night. This will make people think you work 24 hours a day.

4 React when people saying things in meetings. Nod your head, go "hmmm…", bite your lip, purse and smack your lips – make the speaker feel as if their words have made an impact.

5 Never speak in Corporate Jargon or "Business Speak". If you have to speak plainly and directly, then keep it succinct and to the point. The very second your co-workers smell that you have no idea what you're talking about, they'll be out for blood – and, like the sharks that they are, tear you apart.

Signs That You May Be Going Mad

They say you don't need to be mad to work in an office, but it helps. But what if you genuinely are driving yourself mad? Watch out for these symptoms.

1 You call your manager "Mum"

2 You can't remember if today is Tuesday or Wednesday

3 You buy the same super expensive coffee from the same coffee shop every day simply because it's the closest one to your office

4 You can't remember how you got to work

5 You can't remember getting home from work

6 You get angry when someone else uses "your" coffee mug

7 You take only ten minutes for lunch – even though legally you are allowed to take 60 minutes

8 You stay late to finish a piece of work that could easily be done the next day

9 You empathize with your co-workers

10 You have a "work husband or wife"

11 You start getting an early/later train into/from work to avoid the rush hour

12 You bring a plant to work and keep it on your desk. Effectively, you're nesting.

13 You stop buying toilet roll, because you know you can steal it from work

14 You tell your partner that you don't have the "bandwidth" to deal with their problems

15 You start noticing the clothing choices of your colleagues, and how often they wear certain items

Playlist – Tunes To Get You Through Hump Day (Wednesday)

The worst day of the week, Wednesday, often needs a little encouragement to make sure it turns into Thursday. These songs help…

▶ 1. **Here Comes The Sun – The Beatles**

▶ 2. **Hey Ya – Outkast**

▶ 3. **Come On Eileen – Dexy's Midnight Runners**

▶ 4. **Five O' Clock Somewhere – Jimmy Buffett**

▶ 5. **Olivia Newton John – Physical**

▶ 6. **Uptown Funk – Mark Ronson (feat. Bruno Mars)**

▶ 7. **Mardy Bum – Arctic Monkeys**

▶ 8. **Fun, Fun, Fun – Beach Boys**

▶ 9. **Sabotage – Beastie Boys**

▶ 10. **Burn – Ellie Goulding**

Office Dare #7 – Say Why

Say "why" every time someone asks you to do something. Preferably in a whiny child's voice.

Party Poopers

A recent survey of more than 2,000 people aged 25 to 55 discovered that 26% people had regretted something they'd done at the office Christmas party. Regrets range from telling their boss they don't like them to snogging a colleague. What the survey didn't highliight is that the other 74% are liars.

You Know You Work In An Office When...

You'll spend more than 100,000 hours of your life stuck in an office, so you'll be forgiven for going a little stir crazy. But just don't get "instutionalized" like the old guy from *The Shawshank Redemption*. If you do any of the crazy stuff below, it's time to escape to your own Zihuatanejo.

1 You call your husband/ wife the name of the person you sit next to in the office

2 You look forward to doing your expenses form every month

3 You start dressing the same as other people in the office

4 You call your spreadsheets a "work of art"

5 You get that Friday feeling on a Thursday night

6 You get the Monday Blues on a Sunday Night

7 You start your weekend drinking on Tuesday

8 You use "working late again" as an excuse to never go to the gym

9 You find yourself copying the strange behaviours of your co-workers

10 You dream of your boss in a sexually explicit way

Famous People Who Become Famous Later In Life

So what if you're 43 and still assistant to the junior, deputy regional director. These famous people were equally as slow to get their acts together and still hit the big time... and the big bucks.

1. **Susan Boyle, 48**

2. **Harrison Ford, 35**

3. **Christoph Waltz, 51**

4. **Judi Dench, 61**

5. **Bryan Cranston, 44**

6. **Morgan Freeman, 52**

7. **Ricky Gervais, 40**

8. **Samuel L Jackson, 45**

9. **Steve Carrell, 43**

10. **Kathy Bates, 42**

Quote Quota #69

ʿʿ I'm famous for my motivational skills. Everyone always says they have to work a lot harder when I'm around. ʿʿ

Homer Simpson

Office Dare #8 –
Mindlessness At Work

Modern offices are a breeding ground for mindlessness. Make sure you increase your productivity for tedium and monotony every opportunity you have.

You can do this by never spell-checking any of your emails and talking like a robot when anyone ever commands you to do something they think is important.

Office-Related Cocktails – Part 1

Go ahead and make one (or all) of these home-made work-related cocktails, all guaranteed to dull the senses and slow the mind, just as if you were still stuck at your desk staring miserably at your monitor.

iDrink
A potent number to pay tribute to Apple Inc, whose time-wasting apps and tech make the working day a little easier to bear:

1 shot of whisky
1 shot of tequila
1 splash of coke
1 lemon squeeze
1 photo taken on an iPhone 6 and uploaded to
 Instagram

Printer jam
A sweet little treat to get you through an afternoon of photocopying:

2 shots of vodka
1 spoonful of strawberry jam, smoothed around
 the rim of the glass
1 error message (ignored)

The Intern (Non-Alcoholic)
Best to stay clear off:

1 shot of orange juice
1 wheatgrass shot chaser
1 early night

Xmas Party
This cocktail recipe is usually followed by the phrase "I'm never drinking again" the next morning:

3 shots dark rum
5 shots of tequila
2 glugs of someone's unwanted G&T
1 moment of regret

Office Pet Hates #1

We're all human. But some of us turn into animals when we walk through those office doors. Your farts don't stink of roses, I'm sure, but when it comes to pet hates, these people are the worst…

1 People who poke their pens into their ears… then look at what came out… and then eat it!

2 People who fart and then walk out of the office, just in case it's a really smelly one and they don't want to get blamed.

3 People who yawn way too loudly. You're bored, we get it already!

4 People who come to your desk for a chat and then steal your nice pen while they're there.

5 People who pick their nose, because they thinking no one is looking at them, and then eat it.

6 People who bring their pets into work. You own a cute dog? That's awesome. But you're still a scumbag.

Quote Quota #29

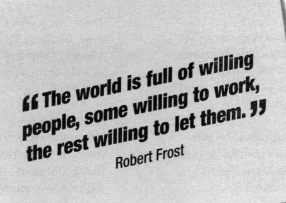

“The world is full of willing people, some willing to work, the rest willing to let them.”

Robert Frost

Office Distractions

There are many things to distract you in an office. Not because they are fun, shiny and fascinating, but because absolutely anything will distract you from having to sit at your desk and check your inbox.

1

A Co-worker's Birthday
In an office of 100 workers, it'll be someone's birthday every four days (on average). Might as well spend quality time with them all on their birthdays!

2

The New Person
There's always a new starter. Get to know them. Take them for lunch, hang out with them all day. Use them to help you not do any work.

3

Leaving Card & Drinks
As one person starts, another leaves. Use your day to meticulously plan someone's leaving drinks party and make their leaving card. Spend all day on it.

Horrible Bosses –
Through History

If you work in an office, then it's 99.8 per cent likely that your boss is a moron. If you are a boss, just be thankful that you're not as hated as these globally despised bosses below who ruined or are ruining the fun for the rest of us.

1. **Adolf Hitler**
2. **Atilla the Hun**
3. **Kim Jong-un**
4. **Osama Bin Laden**
5. **Caligula**
6. **Genghis Khan**
7. **Ivan the Terrible**
8. **Charles Ponzi**
9. **Pol Pot**
10. **Bernie Madoff**

Your Office Is Literally Trying To Kill You Every Day

The air you breathe in your office is up to 100 times dirtier than the air you breathe outside... but sadly that's not the only thing in there that's trying to end your career as a living human being...

1 **Carbon Monoxide** – Look up. See a ventilation duct? That goes straight into a parking lot, where carbon monoxide from all the cars is now being pumped direct into your lungs.

2 **Black mould** – If your building is older than ten years, there will be black mould somewhere. Black mould releases Volatile Organic Chemicals which are toxic to humans – many thousands of office workers die of black mould poisoning worldwide every year.

3 **Ozone** – Do you ever walk over to the office photocopier or printer and think it smells funny? That's ozone and it's killing you. But don't worry: the manufacturers built in a filter to stop the ozone from leaking. When was the last time someone replaced the filter?

4 **Printer toner** – Your colour printer is emitting millions of tiny chemicals of toner into the air. These chemicals enter your bloodstream and lungs and increase your chances of cancer and heart disease. Scientists agree that breathing in toner is as bad as smoking a few cigarettes.

5 **Over-illumination** – Office fluorescent lighting gets a bad rep – and for good reason. It is killing you. Too much bright artificial light messes with our natural sleep cycles. Fluor-

lighting, designed in the 1990s, was placed in most offices, as a way to increase productivity. But it can cause anxiety, migraines, stress, heart attacks and erectile dysfunction.

6 **Motivational Meetings** – Staff "fun" days out, team building exercises, motivational speakers – they are all designed to reinforce a positive attitude for your work and co-workers in the office space. It's bollocks. Scientists have proven that fake positivity is worse for your mental health than genuine negativity and can lead to depression.

7 **Boredom** – Boredom is the worst killer of all. Not only does boredom suck out your life force, increase lethargy and reduce empathy, it also puts you at a higher exposure to heart attack. By turning up, tuning in and dropping off at your dull office job, your heart rate decreases – meaning it won't work effectively when you need it to, such as, running away from the boss. Boredom also increases workplace accidents; your brain goes into autopilot mode, and doesn't react as quickly when you spill boiling hot tea onto your genitals.

8 **Sitting Down** – You're probably reading this sitting down, aren't you? Sitting is one of the most passive things you can do; it burns very few calories. From 9am to 6pm, five days a week – around 100,000-hours of your life – you are putting absolutely no strain on your body whatsoever.

9 **Snacking** – Most office employers snack at least two times a day more than those who work outdoors. Excessive snacking on sugar-rich treats – especially while sitting down – can increase your chances of obesity, diabetes and tooth decay.

10 **Stress** – One in three of us is constantly living with extreme stress, caused by work and money anxieties. Ironically, stressed workers are 10-20 per cent less productive than happy workers. Excessive stress can lead to heart attacks, psychological issues and death (see Karōshi). Get out while you're still alive!

Karoshi

Karōshi, translated literally as "death from overwork" in Japanese, is precisely that – sudden death caused by work. More than 10,000 Japanese works die each year from karōshi, as a result of working more than 70 hours a week. The major medical causes of karōshi deaths are heart attack and stroke due to stress and bad diet. Japanese corporations, weary that their employees seemed to be working themselves to the bone, instigated work schemes with less emphasize on work. Toyota, the car manufacturer, now issues public address announcements at the end of the day, telling staff to go home and be with their loved ones, after the company recognized that employees cannot work for 12 or more hours a day, 6 days a week, year after year, without deteriorating physically and mentally.

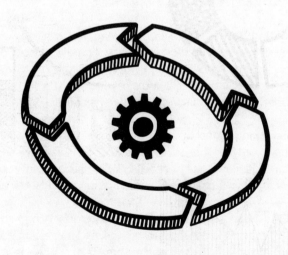

Work Facts

You – yes, you! – are 40 per cent more likely to die than someone who doesn't have an office job. Why? Because you sit down for more than six hours a day and that's very bad for your body. Make sure you stand up and walk around the office every 30 minutes. Alternatively, find a new job, preferably one not stuck in an office.

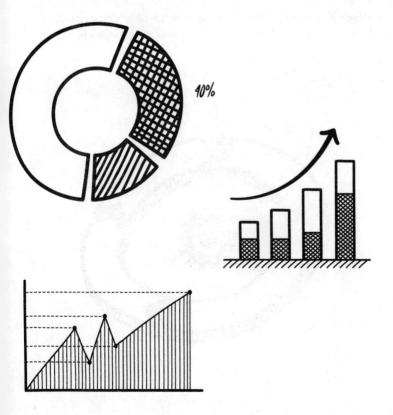

40%

Quote Quota #71

"When a man tells you he got rich through hard work, ask him: 'whose?'"

Don Marquis

Office Pet Hates – Part 2

No matter what industry you're in, or where you do your work, every job has its negative aspects. Strippers may have greasy poles, athletes have nipple sores and captains get hijacked by pirates. But that's nothing compared to office woes like these…

1 People who gossip all the time about other people, in order to make themselves appear more magnificent

2 People who use the microwave in the kitchen, create a mess of atomic-bomb proportions, and then never clean it up

3 People who go out of their way to tell you how busy they are, and how much work they have to do, but then disregard how busy you are when you do the same

4 People who schedule meetings at 09:00 Monday morning

5 People who talk really loudly on the phone, because they think the call is important

6 Forgetting your work fob at home, and then people telling you what an idiot you are all day

7 Doing actual work

Please Wash Your Hands

Sixty-three per cent of all your male co-workers won't have washed their hands after going to the bathroom. Acceptable if it's a No.1, a bit rude if it's a No.2.

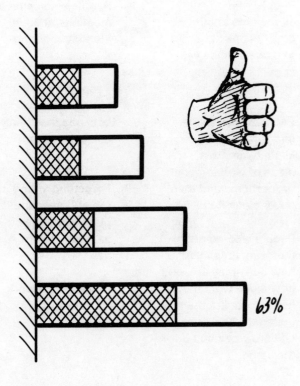

63%

Big Boss, Little Compassion

Your boss, or manager, is no doubt a fountain of knowledge and industry expertise with decades of relevant experience. Below is a helpful guide to the ten things your boss knows about workplace compassion, however:

1.

2.

3.

4.

5.

6.

7.

8.

9.

10.

The Rat Race

We humans are said to think about sex every six seconds – that's ten whole minutes in any eight-hour shift – but that's nothing compared to desert rats who have sex 122 times per hour!

Sleeping Your Way To The Top

Fifteen per cent of women interviewed in a recent survey reported that they have slept with their male boss in order to acclerate their careers. Sadly, no survey data is available for men who have slept with their female bosses, but we estimate that it's around 0%.

Crap Chat

Have you ever been at a networking event, or stuck talking to your bad-breathed boss on a works night out and they keep blabbering and jabbering in *your* earhole about some crap you don't care about? Of course you have. It's part of the job. Sometimes you have to get the big guns out and deploy some seriously smelly chat, the smallest of small talk, to make sure that person never wants to speak to you again for the rest of the night – or any other. These ice-breakers will stop all conversation dead. That's a guarantee. Use them, and watch your victims, all pretend to need the loo at once.

1 If a sardine is more than four inches long, then technically it's a pilchard

2 You need a 13mm spanner to undo an M8 bolt

3 The circumference of the rim of a standard pint glass is just less than twice its height

4 The municipal borough of Richmond, Surrey, was the first local authority in England and Wales to commence a programme of municipal housing provision under the 1890 Housing Act

5 The hairs that grow on your bottom are 50 per cent wider than the ones that grow on your arm

6 Chewing gum while peeling onions will keep you from crying

7 A cow produces 200 times more gas a day than a person

Be More Dutch

With Sweden trialling six-hour working days in 2015, it will be interesting to see what other countries reduce their working week hours in the wake of its impact. Let's hope that a three-day working week becomes the international standard by the year 2020.

1. **Netherlands:** 1,381 hours – **NICE!**

2. **Germany:** 1,397 hours

3. **Norway:** 1,420 hours

4. **France:** 1,479 hours

5. **Denmark:** 1,526 hours

6. **Ireland:** 1,529 hours

7. **Belgium:** 1,574 hours

8. **Luxembourg:** 1,609 hours

9. **Sweden:** 1,621 hours

10. **Slovenia:** 1,640 hours

11. **Switzerland:** 1,636 hours

12. **United States:** 1,654 hours

13. **Finland:** 1,672 hours

14. **Spain:** 1,686 hours

15. **Portugal:** 1,691 hours

16. **Austria:** 1,699 hours

17. **Iceland:** 1,706 hours

18. **New Zealand:** 1,706 hours

19. **Canada:** 1,710 hours

20. Australia: 1,728 hours

21 Japan: 1,746 hours

22. Italy: 1,752 hours

23. Slovak Republic: 1,785 hours,

24. United Kingdom: 1,790 hours

25. Czech Republic: 1,800 hours

26. Turkey: 1,855 hours

27. Hungary: 1,888 hours

28. Estonia: 1,889 hours

29. Israel: 1,910 hours

30. Poland: 1,929 hours

31. Russian Federation: 1,982 hours

32. Chile: 2,029 hours

33. Greece: 2,034 hours

34. Korea: 2,090 hours

35. Mexico: 2,226 hours – **NAUGHTY!**

Source (in case you thought we made it all up): Organisation for Economic Co-operation and Development (OECD)'s Better Life Index, 2015. Figures per year.

Office Treasure Hunt

There's nothing better – save for actually going home – than corralling a load of your co-workers together to compete in the bi-weekly office treasure hunt. These time-wasting beauties are a load of fun, and a great way to show your company just how little you care about the work you do.

Firstly, as Treasure Hunter Co-ordinator, it is your job to divide all the hunters into teams. In order to maximize the length of the treasure hunt, pair up the slow-witted people with the intelligent players. (That way, the clever-clogs won't bunch together.) Once that's done, sit the teams down at their individual desk and tell them to wait for further instructions.

Now, its time to hide the "treasure". Twenty items is a good amount, depending on your office size. Items should range from Miriam's stapler through to Accounts Payable folder 2016 through to your CEO's squash racket. Pride yourself on collecting as many fun bits of treasure as possible. Once completed, go back to your desk and begin writing your clues. Keep it brief but challenging. Use Microsoft Word. The key is to make sure your hunters take all day to find the treasure. Print out the clues for each team. When you're ready, email everyone with the word "GO!" in the subject line. While everyone is off scouring the office, you can think of a great prize to email the winners – biscuits usually suffice.

REMEMBER

When it comes to office treasure hunts it's not about the winning, or the taking part that counts – it's about the time not spent doing any work.

Office Dare #12 –
Stay In Character

Be someone different at work today. Perhaps choose you favourite film character, like Yoda from *Star Wars*, and speak like him for the entire day. It's worth it, if only to have conversations like this with your boss:

Boss **Have you done any work today?**

You **Today try not. Do... or do not. Do I did not. There is no try today. Tomorrow, yes, tomorrow work maybe I.**

Boss **When can I get that spreadsheet I asked for?**

You **Complete soon I will. No sheet spread today though for you. Not need it now you do.**

Boss **Would you mind staying late tonight?**

You **Fear is the path to the dark side, fear leads to anger, anger leads to hate, hate leads to suffering, suffering leads to working late. So no tonight work late, I will.**

Office-Related Cocktails – Part 2

T.G.I.F.
It's Friday lunchtime... time to blow off some steam.

2 pints of lager, at lunchtime
1 glass of white wine, at lunchtime
1 shot of gin
½ as much work done as promised
1.30 train home

Monday Morning Blues
The perfect way to start a crap Monday...

3 shots of gin, mixed with
1 shot of vinegar (to disguise smell of booze)
1 breath mint (to disguise smell of vinegar)

Pay Rise Slammer

Forget the fact that you didn't get a pay rise this year. A Pay Rise Slammer will make you completely forget where you work:

2 shots of tequila
1 shot of vodka
1 shot Ouzo
1 snort of salt
1 lick of honey

Verbal Warning

Three Verbal Warnings and you're out!

2 shots of cognac
2 shots of bourbon
1 glass rim, sweetened with sugar

Day Off

The Day Off is everyone's favourite cocktail, designed to put everyone into a relaxed state of mind.

1 shot of milk
1 shot of dark rum
1 spoonful of honey
1 Valium

Playlist About Not Working Hard

Songs to create spreadsheets to…

- 1. **Can We Fix It? – Bob the Builder**
- 2. **Bang The Drum All Day – Todd Rungren**
- 3. **Five O'Clock World – The Vogues**
- 4. **Got A Job – The Miracles**
- 5. **On My Way to Work – Paul McCartney**
- 6. **Shiftwork – Kenny Chesney**
- 7. **Work Bitch – Britney Spears**
- 8. **We Can Work It Out – The Beatles**
- 9. **Working My Way Back To You – The Four Seasons**
- 10. **The Day The Work Is Done – Take That**

Quote Quota #66

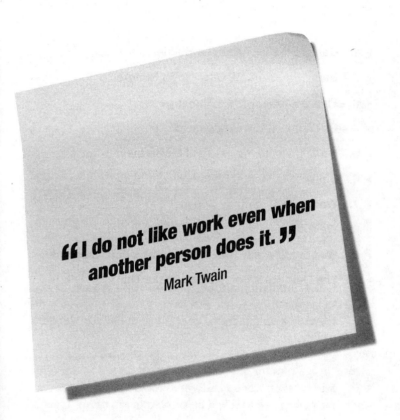

❝ I do not like work even when another person does it. ❞

Mark Twain

Office Dares –
Mind Games

Playing mind games on your colleagues is a hilarious way to inject some hilarity into the hours between 9 and 5, Monday to Friday. These mind games are best played out as "Long Cons" on the same person – can you keep them going the whole week?

1 Call the person you sit next to "Dan"

2 Write "Property of Dan" all over their office stationery

3 Change the clock to 12 minutes previous on your co-worker's computer everyday, before they arrive. By the end of the week, they would have lost a whole hour

4 Make constant tea rounds, three times a day, throughout the week. But always forget to make a drink for the same colleague each time, claiming, "Oh sorry, I forgot about you"

5 Tape a picture of your co-worker onto the underside lid of the photocopier. Every time someone makes a photocopy all that will be printed is his or her face

6 Watch them type their passcode into their smartphone, then when they leave the office without it, change the language settings of their phone to Danish. The look on their face when they return will be *uvurderlige*!

7 Set up a email account name juryselection@gov.uk, and email a co-worker telling them they have been selected for jury duty, starting tomorrow

8 Tell a co-worker that the photocopier is now voice-activated

9 Tell a co-worker they received a phone call, while they were away from their desk, from "someone calling himself the Judge", and that "you have broken a blood oath" and to "watch your back". Then tell them he didn't leave a number to call back on

Office Prank #13 – Keyboard Garden

When your colleague, or boss, goes away for an extended holiday, this is your chance to strike. Go to their desk and extract every letter key from the keyboard, one by one. Once that's done, fill in the holes with garden soil. Now, comes the fun bit. Plant some grass seed into the keyboard and ever-so-slightly water. Pat down the seeds. Shine their desktop lamp onto the keyboard and walk away whistling.

When your colleague arrives back to the office there should be a nice little green patch of newly grown garden lawn waiting for them as a welcome back present.

Shut The Front Door

Excessive swearing in offices is usually not tolerated, but it still happens every now and again when a notification email comes through requesting your presence at yet another unnecessary meeting.

So, instead of effing and blinding like a football hooligan, why not substitute your swearing by shouting this handy little ACRONYM below instead. Your boss will think you are beating yourself up trying to super proactive, but really you're telling everyone in the office precisely what you think of them. Remember, it's all about FOCUS.

F O C U S =

F**K

OFF

COS

UR

STUPID

Office Prank #17 – Air Horn

Buy an air horn, plus air canister from the Internet. Get it delivered to work. Once it arrives, sellotape it under a co-worker's swivel chair. When they sit down, the noise will make their bowels turn to jelly. Priceless.

Hide And Sleep

Hide and Seek is a popular children's game. As you're an adult, and work in an office, why not play Hide and Sleep instead. The rules of the game are simple. Find a place in the office to hide. And sleep. The winner is the player who can't be found between the hours of 09:00 and 17:30.

Playlist About Hardly Working

Songs to chillax out to…

▸ 1. **I'm A Lazy Sod – Sex Pistols**

▸ 2. **The Life of Riley – The Lightning Seeds**

▸ 3. **I Don't Have to Be Me ('Til Monday) – Steve Azar**

▸ 4. **Beats Workin' – Van Halen**

▸ 5. **Lazy Bones – Green Day**

▸ 6. **I'm So Tired – The Beatles**

▸ 7. **Why Don't You Get A Job – The Offspring**

▸ 8. **Chillin Wiv Da Man Dem – Dizzee Rascal**

▸ 9. **I Need To Wake Up – Melissa Etheridge**

▸ 10. **Wake Me Up Before You Go Go – Wham!**

Alternatives To Swearing

Every office worker is complained about at least once in their career and encouraged to reduce their swearing so as not to offend other people's "delicate sensibilities". While most managers realize the importance of their employee's expressing themselves freely, it has become "corporate policy" at many international companies to try an innovative approach to swearing, using alternative phrases. The table below highlights some of the most commonly used examples:

INSTEAD OF	TRY SAYING
You don't know what the f**k you are doing	Do you know what you're doing?
She's a total, ball-busting mega bitch	She's an ambitious overachiever
When the f**k do you expect me to do this?	I'll work late then, I guess
No f**king way!	I believe that is unfair
You've got to be sh*tting me!	Really? How very odd
I don't give a sh*t!	That's someone else's problem
Not my f**k ing problem	Nothing to do with me
What the f**k?	That's interesting. Tell me more
This sh*t won't work	I'm not sure this is a valid request
Don't waste my f**k ing time	This will take longer than you expect
He's got his head up his arse	He's not aware of the issues
Eat sh*t, you idiot	Excuse me, what did you say?
Shove the job up your arse	I don't think you understand
This job sucks	I love a challenge
My boss has just f**k ed me in the arse	My boss is a pain in the bottom

Orwellian Tea

In 1946, the famed writer of the literary masterpiece *1984*, George Orwell, wrote an essay about his 11 rules for making the perfect cup of tea. As an office worker you're used to following stupid rules – but how many of these do you actually follow?

"When I look through my own recipe for the perfect cup of tea I find no fewer than eleven outstanding points. Here are my own eleven rules, every one of which I regard as golden:"

1 Always use Indian tea. "the phrase 'a nice cup of tea' invariably means Indian tea."

2 Tea should be made in small quantities — that is, "in a teapot

3 The pot should be warmed beforehand.

4 The tea should be strong. "I maintain that one strong cup of tea is better than twenty weak ones."

5 The tea should be poured straight into the pot.

6 Take the teapot to the kettle and not the other way about.

7 After making the tea, one should stir it, "or better, give the pot a good shake."

8 Drink out of a good breakfast cup.

9 You should pour the cream off the milk before using it for tea.

10 Pour tea into the cup first. "By putting the tea in first and stirring as one pours, one can regulate the amount of milk"

11 No sugar. "How can you call yourself a true tea lover if you destroy the flavour by putting sugar in it

Office Prank #14 – Out Of Order

An oldie but a goodie. This is a classic office prank.

1) **Print out a sheet of A4 with the words' "OUT OF ORDER" printed on it, in Comic Sans MS font, naturally.**

2) **Now, tape this sign to anything – toilet doors, printers, photocopiers, your bosses door, the ceiling – everything.**

3) **Watch the office descend into beautiful chaos.**

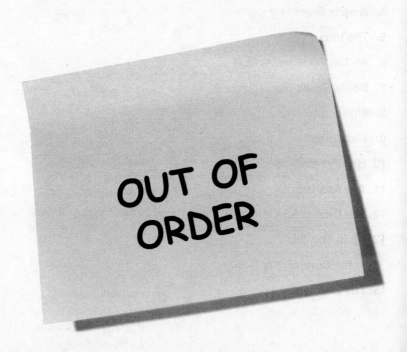

Top 15 Movies That Are Set In The Workplace

Movies are a great way to suspend our disbelief, believe in magic, and escape from the dull monontony of our daily routines of office life. But, for some bizarre reason, we also love to watch movies that are set in offices. It's as if we can't get enough of punishing ourselves! If you haven't seen them, these classic movies are a must. Don't forget to watch them at work, for that added sense of reality…

1. **Office Space**

2. **Glengarry Glen Ross**

3. **Broadcast News**

4. **Nine to Five**

5. **The Intern**

6. **All The President's Men**

7. **Boiler Room**

8. **Working Girl**

9. **Wall Street**

10. **Horrible Bosses**

11. **The Apartment**

12. **The Devil Wears Prada**

13. **Up In The Air**

14. **In the Company of Men**

15. **The Internship**

Office One Liners

Sneak these witty one-liners in next time you need to sound clever at work...

1. A clean desk is a sign of a cluttered desk drawer.

2. If at first you don't succeed, redefine success.

3. A thing not worth doing isn't worth doing well.

4. If a thing is worth doing, it would have been done already.

5. The floggings will continue until morale improves.

6. I don't have a solution, but I do admire the problem.

7. Many people quit looking for work when they find a job.

8. Bureaucrats cut red tape, lengthwise.

9. Forty-three per cent of all statistics are made up.

10. A committee is a group of people who individually can do nothing, but as a group decide that nothing can be done.

Quote Quota #99

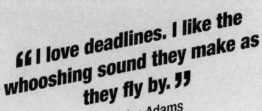

❝I love deadlines. I like the whooshing sound they make as they fly by. ❞

Douglas Adams

Office Bantz #1

I thought I saw a light at the end of the tunnel, but it was only some moron with a torch bringing me more work.

Office-opoly

Bored? Of course you are. Why not create your own Office version of the popular board game Monopoly then? Print your own money, devise your own board rules, and use items such as paperclips, and pen-tops as player pieces. Collect £200 every time you pass Go, and don't stop until everyone has bought hotels on delux office space, or is completely broke. The longer the game the better – why not see if you can keep a game going for a whole week?

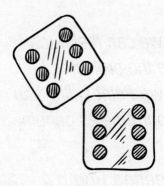

Office Prank #15 – Advertise Your Next Meeting

Photocopy this sign, below, and pin it to the company noticeboard.

ARE YOU LONELY?

Tired of working on your own?
Do you hate making decisions?

COME TO MY NEXT MEETING!

Together we can feel important, eat biscuits, use the projector, be impressed with our PowerPoint skills, and disguise wasting our time as genuine work!

*Go To Meeting Room A – **NOW!***

Office Bantz #2

A popular office joke for you...

"This is the story about four people named Everybody, Somebody, Anybody, and Nobody. There was an important job to be done and Everybody was sure that Somebody would do it. Anybody could have done it, but nobody did it. Somebody got angry about that, because it was Everybody's job. Everybody thought that anybody could do it, but Nobody realized that Everybody wouldn't do it. It ended up that Everybody blamed Somebody, when Nobody did what Anybody could of done."

In Case Of Emergency

This useful destress kit, below, wlll help keep you on the right side of sanity. Use only once.

1. **Place this page on a firm surface. Feel free to print out.**
2. **Follow directions in circle below**
3. **Repeat until you are destressed or become unconscious**

BANG HEAD HERE

Office Hack #1

Need a tripod for your iPhone so you can watch a movie at your desk while you're boss is away?

Easy. Get two binder clips, insert your business card between them and then slot your smartphone in between the clips. Job done.

Office Hack #2

Sick of loose cables and long wires getting entangled under your feet or on your desk? A great way to tidy them up is to use [drum roll, please] toilet rolls. Fold and overlap the cables into the toilet rolls and voilà – no more f**king long wires tripping you up every time you get up from your desk.

The Humble Office Mug

The office mug has contributed a lot to office morale over the years, as the container that delivers hot, refreshing beverages. But, recently, the office mug has served to deliver another purpose – the witty slogan. Have you seen any of these mugs used by any mugs recently?

1. I love marketing!
2. Spreadsheet users do it in cells
3. World's Best Boss
4. I hate mugs with funny slogans on
5. Just say no to meetings
6. Keep Calm and Continue Working
7. I am the most stressed person in the office
8. Is it Friday yet?
9. I'm not a morning person
10. Office Hottie

Motivational Work Slogans

Some companies hang motivational slogans around the office. They're there to make you work harder. Feel free to print these ones off – and then graffiti them with penis doodles.

Dreams don't work unless you do

ALL ROADS THAT LEAD TO SUCCESS HAVE TO PASS THROUGH HARD WORK BOULEVARD AT SOME POINT

If you want to make something for yourself, work harder than everybody else

Imagine. Believe. Achieve.

Winners are not people who never fail, but people who never quit

Every day may not be good, but there is something good in every day

ATTITUDE IS EVERYTHING

Every accomplishment starts with the decision to try

Work harder than you think you did yesterday

KEEP CALM AND CARRY ON

Evil Companies In Movies

Your company may be unethical, tyrannical and employ incompetent micro-managers, but just be thankful it's not quite as bad as these guys:

1. **Weyland-Utani Corporation,** *Aliens*

2. **Umbrella Corporation,** *Resident Evil*

3. **InGen Inc.,** *Jurassic Park*

4. **Multi-National United (MNU),** *District 9*

5. **Tyrell Corporation,** *Blade Runner*

6. **Engulf and Devour Corporation,** *Silent Movie*

7. **Cyberdyne Systems,** *Terminator 2: Judgment Day*

8. **Initech,** *Office Space*

9. **Soylent Corporation,** *Soylent Green*

10. **RDA Corporation,** *Avatar*

11. **Spectre,** as often encountered by James Bond

12. **Omni Consumer Products,** *Robocop*

13. **Rekall,** *Total Recall*

14. **BiffCo,** *Back To The Future II*

15. **Energy Corporation,** *Rollerball*

16. **LexCorp,** *Superman Returns*

17. **Buy n Large,** *Wall-E*

18. **Cloverleaf Industries,** *Who Framed Roger Rabbit*

19. **The Trade Federation,** *Star Wars I, II, III*

20. **Enron,** *Enron: The Smartest Guys In The Room*

Quote Quota #44

> **❝ Work is just another of man's diseases and prevention is better than the cure. If you don't look for work, work won't look for you. ❞**
>
> Heathcote Williams

Office Prank #16 – Roll With It

On every square of the toilet roll, in one of the office cubicles, write this message:

WHOEVER PULLS THE FINAL SHEET

FROM THIS TOILET ROLL

WINS THEMSELVES A LITTLE TREAT

UNRAVEL ME TO FIND OUT MORE

Now, unravel the whole toilet roll and on the last sheet of paper write your name and a prize. The lucky winner will then come to you, with the final sheet, whereupon you will bestow upon them a great prize.

Rebel Against The Cause

The Man, The Boss, authority, whatever you call it – aren't you fed up of being controlled by it? Don't be a puppet for The Man anymore! Watch these films for inspiration, fight the good fight – and beat The Man at his own game, playing by your own rules.

1. *Ferris Bueller's Day Off*

2. *Rebel Without A Cause*

3. *School of Rock*

4. *The Wild One*

5. *Footloose*

6. *The Hunger Games*

7. *The Outsiders*

8. *1984*

9. *The Double*

10. *Fahrenheit 451*

Reasons We Hate Going To Work, Part 1

Every office is the same, no matter where in the world you live, so I'm pretty certain these items below are familiar to you. They are the real reasons everybody hates going to their office.

1 Noisy typers

2 Noisy eaters

3 Having awkward conversations in lifts/kitchens/corridors/stairwells/anywhere

4 Walking into kitchens that look like a bomb has hit it

5 Walking into toilets and seeing a massive unflushable floater staring back at you

6 Telling everyone on Monday how much fun your weekend was

7 Listen to people bang on about how busy they are all the time

8 Telling infectious people with colds that they should go home

9 Birthday whip-a-rounds

10 Invitations to after work drinks and running out of excuses to say "no"

Office Hack #4

Is your keyboard grimy and dirty? Probably. The best way to clean it without having to stand up is using the sticky side of a Post-it note, or a strip of sellotape, to attract the unwanted lint and dirt.

Reasons We Hate Going To Work, Part 2

The list goes on...

1 Your own birthday drinks party

2 People who ignore important emails

3 People who don't spell check their emails at all

4 Meetings that go on for hours, and you're not sure why you're even there

5 People who hum, whistle and suck through their teeth at their desk

6 People who bring their babies to work

7 Corporate jargon infiltrating your conversations at home

8 Co-workers who don't know how to use technology

9 Co-workers who never refill the paper tray in printers

10 Co-workers who send you emails – when they sit right next to you

Quote Quota #58

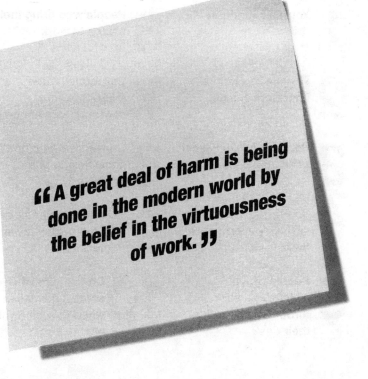

" A great deal of harm is being done in the modern world by the belief in the virtuousness of work. "

Rise Of The Zombie

Lately, it seems like every time we turn on the TV, or surf the Internet there is a new zombie-related TV show or movie. It's as if TV executives who commission this sh*t know that we are lifeless zombies ourselves, thanks to our robot-drone roles at brain-chewing corporations that are quite literally sucking the life out of us – and we swallow it up like the sheep we are.

1. *iZombie*

2. *Zombieland*

3. *Z Nation*

4. *The Walking Dead*

5. *Fear The Walking Dead*

6. *World War Z*

7. *Shaun Of The Dead*

8. *Dead Set*

9. *Warm Bodies*

10. *The Returned*

Reasons We Hate Going To Work, Part 3

...And on...

1 People who eat salads for lunch

2 People who cycle to work

3 People who go for lunchtime runs

4 People who eat healthy snacks

5 Co-workers who never make tea or coffee for anyone except themselves

6 Work appraisals

7 Colleagues who tell you how stressed they are – all the time

8 Working to a deadline with a hangover

9 Time passing ridiculously slowly

10 Introducing yourself to the New Guy

Office Hack #5

If your laptop works as hard as you do, then why not help it out.

Cut an empty egg box in half and place it under your laptop to stop the computer from overheating... and from hearing the fan constantly straining to breathe – a sound that is akin to Darth Vader choking on his own Force-strangle.

David Brentisms

Everyone's favourite manager-entertainer is full of advice that every office worker should follow. Here's five of his very best:

1 "A problem shared is a problem halved, so is your problem really yours or just half of someone else's?"

2 "You have to be 100% behind someone, before you can stab them in the back."

3 "If work was so good, the rich would have kept more of it for themselves."

4 "If your boss is getting you down, look at him through the prongs of a fork and imagine him in jail."

5 "If you can keep your head when all around you have lost theirs, then you probably haven't understood the seriousness of the situation."

Reasons We Hate Going To Work, Part 4

And on...

1 Catching people's eyes looking at you from over your computer monitor

2 Waiting for the smell to dissipate after an odorous visit to the toilet

3 Colleagues who don't clean mugs properly

4 Colleagues speaking loudly to other workers on Skype

5 Colleagues who stand next to your desk while you're on the phone

6 Colleagues who don't replace empty toilet rolls

7 Colleagues who ignore their ringing phone

8 Colleagues who leave their smartphone on their desks, and don't switch it to silent

9 Colleagues who hate Mondays, more than any other day

10 Colleagues who turn up late to meetings, so they have to start again

Job Title Generator

The office is the only workplace in the world where you are legally allowed – nay, it's your duty – to sex up your boring job title into something a lot more dazzling for your CV. To your disappointed parents you may just be a desk donkey and wave slave, but for perspective employers why not add a bit more dazzle to your boring daily roles?

1   **Data entry**   Computer Remuneration Assistant

2   **Answering the telephone**   Telecommunication Executive

3   **Dish Washer**   Crockery Cleansing Operative

4   **Post-room worker**   Dispatch Services Facilitator

5   **Tidying the office**   Environment Improvement Technician

6 **Filling in for Reception** Frontline Customer Liaison

7 **Lifting boxes** Resource Operative

8 **Putting the bins out** Waste management and Disposal Technician

9 **Making the tea** Refreshment Coordinator

10 **Filing** Storage Assistant

11 **Photocopying stuff** File Duplication Assistant

12 **Setting up invoices** Payment Facilitator

Reasons We Hate Going To Work, Part 5

And on...

1 Colleagues who fiddle with the heating

2 Colleagues who pick their nose and then look around to see who saw them do it

3 Colleagues who send viral videos, three years after they were first viral

4 Colleagues who arrange meetings on Monday morning

5 Colleagues who arrange meetings on Friday afternoon

6 Colleagues who arrange meetings just before lunchtime

7 Colleagues who arrange meetings

8 Colleagues who all-staff email the whole company about their missing f**king mug

9 Being a grown adult and having to hide in the toilets to avoid doing work

10 Having to eat the relentless amount of birthday cake

Office Buzzwords To Avoid, Part 1

Let's all go out of our way to strangle the following words before they become a thing:

1. Solutionize
2. Thought huddles
3. Clarity chat
4. Synergy strategy
5. Technical grouphug
6. Forward facing
7. Bring to the table
8. Exit strategizing
9. Clear shots on goal
10. Brandifying

Reasons We Hate Going To Work, Part 6

And on...

1 Passive-aggressive note leavers

2 People who come to your desk and steal your pens

3 Colleagues who ask you what you're having for lunch, while you're eating it

4 Having to make everyone else tea or coffee, even though you don't drink either

5 Co-workers who ask for a really complicated drink when it's your turn to make tea

6 Arranging your holiday ten months in advance just to get those days off before anyone else snags them

7 Knowing you could (and do) do a better job than your boss (who gets paid more than you)

8 Having restrained passive-aggressive conversations with co-workers rather than telling the truth

9 Agreeing with someone who is quite obviously wrong

10 Feeling guilty about taking a day off ill, when you are actually sick, but no one will believe it anyway

Quote Quota #3

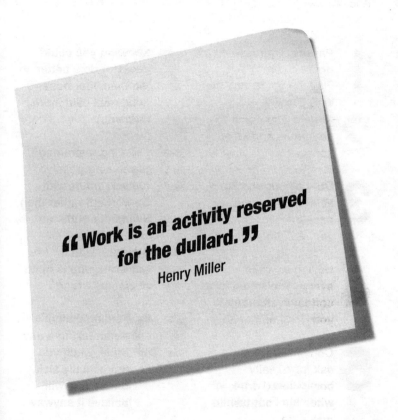

" Work is an activity reserved for the dullard. "
Henry Miller

How To Win At Office Politics

If you're determined to make the most out of your time between 9 and 5, then follow these 20 golden rules to office politicking, below:

1 Play the game/play the long game

2 Form alliances, gather an army

3 Take all the credit, even when there is none to take

4 Manipulate the weak, eradicate the gullible

5 Show favouritism and play favourites

6 Flatter everyone, adore no one

7 Schmooze and network at every opportunity

8 Learn to read people's tells

9 Admit your mistakes, before others point them out

10 Backstab those in your way

11 Spread false rumours

12 Scheme and lie to get what you want

13 Never accept "no", never say "no"

14 Choose your battles

15 Spend time and befriend senior staff outside of work

16 Keep a paper trail / Remember other people's mistakes

17 Don't get embroiled in petty fights

18 Never appear to have a personal life

19 Appear humble to those who can help you

20 Keep a positive mental attitude at all times

Reasons We Hate Going To Work, Part 7

Still going strong…

1 Colleagues who make bad cups of tea or coffee

2 Colleagues who put headphones on, but you can hear still the music loudly

3 Colleagues who always leave ten minutes earlier than everyone else

4 Casual Fridays

5 Colleagues who don't like having the window open (despite it being a hot day)

6 Having to re-do a file after not saving the original

7 An unknown quantity that has stopped your computer from working

8 Fire drills that no one takes seriously

9 Colleagues who eat breakfast at their desk, for what seems like hours

10 Redundancy scares

More Office Buzzwords To Avoid

Just when you thought we'd included way too many buzzword entries in this book, along comes another one. But don't complain. we're just trying to educate you on these things. It's not our fault there are so many buzzwords out there. It's your bosses.

1. **Win-win**
2. **Streamline**
3. **High-order thinking**
4. **Brain break**
5. **Bandwidth**
6. **Bizmeth**
7. **Profit center**
8. **Make it pop**
9. **Mindsharing**
10. **Trending**

Reasons We Hate Going To Work, Part 8

You still with us?

1 Finding out someone who does the same job as you, gets paid more

2 Someone steals your ergonomical chair over the weekend

3 You can hear rats in the skirting boards

4 Your job makes you realize you picked the wrong career

5 Your job makes you realize you have no idea what you're doing

6 You work in Swindon

7 Your commute to work takes two hours each way

8 Training days (taught by someone who has never worked in an office)

9 Realizing your company is nowhere near as cool as others

10 Being asked out on a date by the office weasel

Reasons We Hate Going To Work, Part 9

Nearly there…

1 Getting caught updating your CV by a co-worker

2 Forced conversations about "what you'd do with a million dollars"

3 Being forced to part of the "Office Christmas Party Organization Team"

4 Realizing you have become a cliché of your personality type

5 Coming to grips with the fact you are no longer the office hottie/hunk

6 Having to ask for a raise, because no-one else will do it for you

7 Dealing with hypochondriacs

8 Complaining about a co-worker to HR – and them saying their "hands are tied to do anything about it"

9 Being a part of office politics even though you don't agree

10 The slow realization that you have been at that company for way too long

11 Sitting at your desk after two weeks' vacation sitting on a beach in [insert exotic location]

The Importance Of Being Idle, Part 1

Getting bored – it'll happen at least ten times a day. So here's a handy little To Do list for when boredom creeps into you mind and strangles your thoughts.

1 Write a list of all things you'd buy if you had £10 million in the bank

2 Write a chronological list of everyone you've ever kissed and slept with

3 Write a Pros and Cons list about your partner

4 Write your Christmas Cards, even if it's March

5 Write a handwritten letter to an elderly relative

6 Write a will and testament

7 Write a list of all the people you hate and what they did to piss you off

8 Rank all your friends in order of preference

9 Write a Pros and Cons list about yourself. Email it to your partner

10 Create an alter ego. Then create an online dating profile

Quote Quota #89

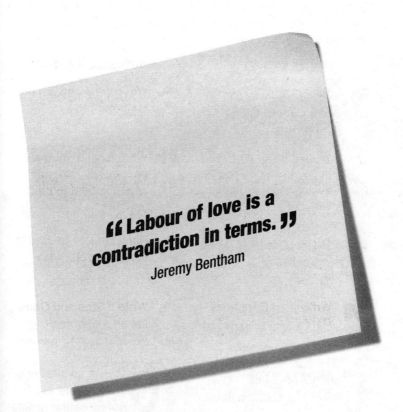

❝ Labour of love is a contradiction in terms. ❞
Jeremy Bentham

Reasons We Hate Going To Work, Part 9

The end...

1 Lying on your CV about how long you've worked there, just to make it seem longer than it feels

2 Sales conferences in Swindon

3 Bitching about work and other co-workers to co-workers on a work night out

4 Seeing people getting sent flowers to their desk on Valentine's Day, and feeling sad/guilty about not receiving/sending any

5 Knowing people stay late, and feeling guilty about not doing that yourself

6 Working out whether anyone actually cares about your Internet history

7 Wearing fancy clothes to work, lying about why, and then sneaking out for a job interview because you don't want to take the day off

8 Being stuck in an office on a hot summer's day

9 Being stuck in an office when it's snowing outside

Office Buzzwords To Avoid, Part 3

Though making fun of buzzwords for being stupid is a bit redundant (something you'll be soon), there is just something about these particular quirks of jargon that make us want to throttle our own throats.

1. Data dump
2. Clickbait
3. Internet of things
4. Cross-platform
5. Fuzzy logic
6. Folksonomy
7. Dot bomb
8. Netiquette
9. Game changer
10. Datafication

Worst Personality Types In An Office

The worst – and I mean *the worst* – thing about working in an office is not that these personality types exist in an office, but the fact that no matter how hard you try, your colleagues have definitely got you tagged as at least one of them. So, which is it?

1 The micromanager

2 The workaholic

3 The kiss-ass

4 The stresshead

5 The cool guy

6 The boss's son/ daughter

7 The office gossip

8 Mr Motivated

9 The super-ambitious

10 The egomaniac

11 The nice but dim

12 The panicker

13 The wisecracker

14 The person with the annoying laugh

15 The person you wouldn't trust further than you could throw them

Office Buzzwords To Avoid, Part 4

Just when you thought it was safe to open your mouth again, along come even more dread-inducing phrases. A single utterance of one of these moronic words in a staff meeting can cause blood pressures to raise by 87 per cent.

1. Incentivize
2. Touch base
3. Loop back
4. On my radar
5. Pre-prepare
6. Conversate
7. Action that
8. Job done
9. 2.0
10. Flat pack the solution

Hilarious Email Signatures

If you absolutely must send work emails from your iPhone or smartphone on a weekend just to prove to your colleagues that you are working, may I suggest changing your email signatures to one of these hilarious alternatives, just so when the recipient receives a work email from you at 1.00am, it will make them at least laugh and not despise you:

1 iPhone. iTypos. iApologize.

2 Typed on tiny keys, just for you

3 Something really small like this so people squint to read it

4 Not sent from my iPhone

5 Don't you just hate it when people try to be funny on their email signatures?

6 You've won a prize, <u>click here</u>

7 "Twenty years from now you will be more disappointed by the things that you didn't do than by the ones you did do. So throw off the bowlines. Sail away from the safe harbor. Catch the trade winds in your sails. Explore. Dream. Discover." *Mark Twain*

8 I'm working – are you?

9 Sent from the future

10 Sent from my iDrone

The Importance Of Being Idle, Part 2

Work doesn't have to be devoid of all fun. Introduce these quirky elements into your day, and who knows, you may just get out of the day alive...

1 Choose a new walking style every time you leave your desk. Exit the office in glorious style.

2 Write a musical about the roles you perform at work. Showtune titles must include 'Error Message 101', 'You Have Been Disconnected From The Server' and 'Spinning Wheel Of Death'.

3 Alert everyone that you are going to the toilet, and specify Number One or Number Two.

4 Start a rubber band ball. Don't stop until it's bigger than your fist.

5 Make a daisy chain out of paper clips. Don't stop until it reaches the ground from the highest window.

6 Suggest a hot-dog eating competition at lunch. First Prize is a can of hot dogs.

7 Come to work in your pyjamas and pretend you are sleepwalking for the whole day.

8 Ask your boss for an appraisal. This always kills time.

9 Take up smoking. Go for a cigarette break.

10 Write a film script loosely based on events that happen in the office. Once the script is finished, hand it to your manager for their thoughts.

Office Hack #6

Got a cold at work? Are people complaining about 9,000 balled-up snotty tissues on your desk? If so, buy two boxes of tissues. Take all the tissues out of one box and put them in the other. Then keep the empty box for all your snot rags. Tie the boxes together with an elastic band, so you can keep and store them together.

Office Hack #7

Is the top drawer of your desk full of pens, paperclips, elastic bands, pins, Post-it notes, etc., running loose and chaotic? If so, why not use mini cereal boxes (with one side cut off) to keep things separate and organized? That way, when you need an elastic band, you don't have to search through a vast collection of erasers to find one.

Office Dares #19 – Write A Theme Tune For The Office

No office is complete without a theme tune. Spend the day writing lyrics about your fellow colleagues, download Garageband app (or any music software available) onto your smartphone and compose a jaunty upbeat melody – or macabre downbeat ballad – that perfectly sums up life in your office. Here are some sample lyrics, to help you on your way…

This is our office
it's a place where things are neat
And Jenny in accounts,
with boobs that always bounce,
makes going upstairs
such a treat

There's lovely Dan in marketing
in fact there's two
there's always a guy called Dan
in every office
and that's just the truth

The boss is a meathead
who hasn't a clue
got a degree in Leisure Management
in 2002
Everyone hates him
for everything that he says
his LinkedIn picture profile
makes him look like a frog

And so on...

Quote Quota #33

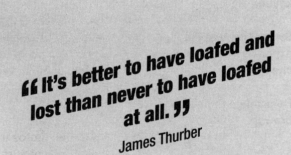

❝ It's better to have loafed and lost than never to have loafed at all. ❞

James Thurber

Office Dares #20 – Fun Shui

While the art of Feng Shui is not as trendy as it was a decade ago, the organization of people's furniture and desk space in their cubicle or office is important to them. Choose a fussy colleague and make it your aim this week to mix up their Feng Shui business:

1 Swap their mouse so it's always on the other side of the keyboard

2 Swap their fancy, expensive pens with cheap biros

3 Re-arrange their desk drawer

4 Use their desk as a dumping ground for textbooks, folders and dead stationery

5 Rub dirt into their keyboard

6 Steal the batteries out of their mouse

7 Steal staples from their stapler. Make sure it's always empty

8 Put a poster up that says "You're a loser" – make sure it's in their eyeline every time they look up from their computer

9 Swap the photos in their family picture frame with images of porn stars you've printed off the Internet

10 Turn off their computer every time they go for lunch, so they have to re-open everything when they return back

All Up In Your Business

Backstabbing your co-workers, so that they never get promoted above you, is easy to do in an office. And fun! There's no "I" in team, remember. Here's how to do it:

1 **Keep a tally of who comes in late every day, then anonymously email the list to your manager**

2 **Spread a rumour alleging that that person to whom you are spreading the rumour is disliked by another employee**

3 Agree with everything they say publically, but denounce their ideas when in private with their manager

4 When the need to fart comes up, walk over to their desk, drop the bomb, then leave. Then complain about the smell from the other side of the room

5 Invite everyone else to lunch and work drinks, except one person. Rotate who that person is, so that you can gossip about everyone, but no one can gossip about you

6 Get everyone to endorse you publicly on LinkedIn. And then never repay the favour

7 When co-workers go on vacation, orchestrate a campaign of hate towards them and their work.

8 Take credit for other people's ideas when they are not in the room, but only give yourself credit for the "initial idea ... everything else was up to them"

Commuter Hell

Look out for these other office drones who will get in your way on your way to the office:

1 Those who get on, and then shout "Move down", on already crushed train carriages.

2 Those who roll their eyes and make that "tsk" noise when someone shouts "move down" at them.

3 Lycra louts on bikes who think they're Lance Armstrong and smugly think the roads belong to them

4 People whose hot breath you can feel on your neck

5 People who jam the doors of Underground carriages and make the rest of us late

6 Train drivers with a cheery disposition

7 Bus drivers who don't stop even though the bus isn't full

8 People who listen to music on their smartphones but don't wear headphones

9 People who look over your shoulder when you're sending a text

10 People who look elderly berate you when you give up your seat for them, when actually they're not that old, and they don't need to sit down

Office Dare #21 – Sellotape Selfie

Find some Sellotape. Wrap it around your head. Make sure your forehead is stretched back, your hair is sticking up, your eyes are bulbous, your nose is squashed, your mouth is mangled and your tongue is out. Take a selfie. Email to everyone at work and ask him or her to beat it. The selfie that looks the most demented wins a prize.

Google Map It

In your darkest, most bored moments, be honest you love nothing more than Google mapping your own house in street view. Well, let's take this idea one step further. Let's look up the world's funniest place names and have a sniff around in street view.

1. **Intercourse,** Pennsylvania, USA

2. **F*cking,** Austria

3. **Hell,** Norway

4. **Dildo,** Canada

5. **Twatt,** Scotland

6. **MIddelfart,** Denmark

7. **Muff,** Ireland

8. **Titty Hill Farm,** UK

9. **Anus,** France

10. **Bastardo,** Perugia, Italy

How To Get The Sack, Part 1

Getting fired isn't as easy as you think. You've got to really think outside the box these days if you want to get the sack. Which is ironic, isn't it?

1 Sell office supplies and stationery on eBay

2 Burn CDs of movies you've downloaded illegally at work (using work DVD-Rs) and sell them to your colleagues

3 Leave the office every day with your bag packed with toilet rolls, teabags, A4 paper, laptops – anything you can sell at a Car Boot Sale

4 Request that people only refer to you as "Super"

5 Start wearing the exact same clothes as your boss, and copy everything he does

6 Buy a new kitchen, on expenses

7 Pretend to throw up in your mouth every time you hear corporate jargon

8 Organize meetings and then never show up

9 Send your boss selfies of you at a theme park, or down a pub, after you called in "sick"

10 Show up to work every other weekday

11 Start bringing a dog to work – it can be a different dog every day

12 Start growing marijuana on your desk. This becomes apparent only when the plant is in full bloom

Quote Quota #128

❝ What I don't like about office Christmas parties is looking for a job the next day. ❞

Phyllis Diller

How To Get The Sack, Part 2 – Live Tweet Your Day

Social media is ruining all our lives one tweet at a time, but it can sometimes come in handy. If you want to get sacked from your sh*tty office job, then this is the quickest and easiest way. Start tweeting your own company's Twitter account with live tweets about how little you are accomplishing that day. Here are a few examples to get you started:

Arrived late this morning. Thinking about watching The Godfather in the toilet before starting any work. Love my job!
@company

Boss is away today. The mice will play. Three-hour lunch! #boozeup
@company

*This place is soooooooooo sh*t!*
@company

Biggest. Poo. Ever. #floater*
@company

*include photo attachment

How To Survive An Office Job

If it's your first day in an office, don't panic, just remember these guidelines and you'll be just fine...

1. **Nothing really matters**

2. **Nobody really cares**

3. **What's the worst that could happen?**

4. **There's always tomorrow**

5. **Everybody makes mistakes**

6. **At the end of the day, nobody died**

7. **Always look on the bright side**

8. **It's just a job**

9. **There's a 1 per cent chance you could die in your sleep**

10. **Rome wasn't built in a day**

How To Poo At Work

If you work in an office where toilet cubicles are at a premium right after breakfast and directly after lunch, and you don't want people to hear your plopping, splashing and grunting, then don't worry, this is how to avoid the embarrassment:

1 Eat out of sync with everyone else – that way, your bowel movement schedule will not align with anyone else's.

2 Always use a toilet on a different floor. That way, co-workers won't know that you're the one in there making all the noise.

3 Every office has a secret bathroom. Find it. Use it. Keep quiet about it..

4 Tell your colleagues you're in a "meeting room making a call", then pop to the loo. Nobody will be suspicious of your absence and nobody will notice when you stroll back in 45 minutes later.

5 Try to minimize your poo-ing to under ten minutes. Unless your book is really good.

6 Lay a few pieces of toilet roll in the waterbowl. This will suppress the sound of the poo hitting the water like a bomb. It acts like a silencer on a gun. Sort of.

7 Have an escape plan ready. Know which exit to use. Don't go to the sink with the empty soap dispenser. Remember always be poo-prepared.

8 Buy some fake legs from Amazon. Put them in the stalls opposite you. When people walk in, they'll see all the stalls are occupied and leave you in peace.

9 Go to a nearby restaurant and poo there.

10 Be proud of your poo. Be confident of your grunting, and let your poo plop with panache. Don't be afraid to poo if there's someone in the other cubicle. If anyone looks horrified at you, just tell him or her, "it's a part of life – GET OVER IT", and storm out. After washing your hands, of course.

Can't You See I'm Busy

How to waste time at work more time-effectively. Off you go…

1. **Plan your next holiday in meticulous detail**
2. **Diagnose that rash on WebMd or NHS.co.uk**
3. **Cull those 450 Facebook friends who are not your friends**
4. **Learn another language**
5. **Create a completely original CV**
6. **Take a free online course**
7. **Take an IQ Test**
8. **Delete "friends" on Facebook**
9. **Check your MySpace account**
10. **Start a blog about how boring your job is, and update it every half hour with the things you didn't do since the last time you blogged**

Awkward Puns

Depending on who you speak to, and how your mother raised you, puns are either the spawn of Lucifer or the greatest thing since sliced bread. In an office, puns are inevitable, once all meaningful conversation has broken down. They are candied about like M&Ms (see what I did there?). In order to survive, why not have these amazing puns ready to use for your next awkward kitchen conversation; they'll make you sound ever-so witty.

1 I tried to catch some fog once. I mist

2 I once stayed up all night to see where the sun went. Then it dawned on me

3 I'm reading a book about anti-gravity. I can't put it down

4 They told me I had Type A blood, but it was a Type-O

5 When chemists die, they barium

6 How does Moses make his tea? Hebrews it

7 This girl said she recognized me from the vegetarian club, but I'd never met herbivore

8 When you get a bladder infection, urine trouble

9 I know a guy who's addicted to brake fluid. He says he can stop any time

10 I didn't like my beard at first. Then it grew on me

11 I wondered why the football was getting bigger. Then it hit me!

Problem Solving Flow Chart

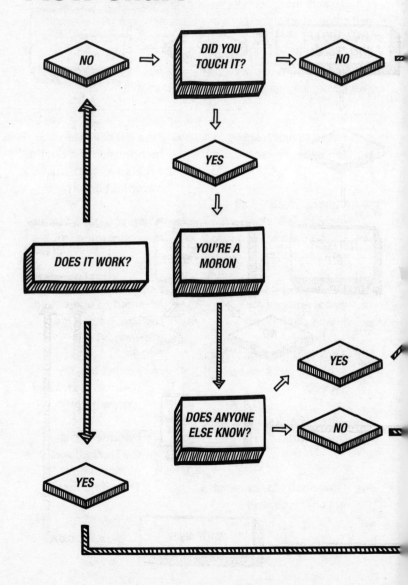

If you work in an office, chances are you've got a few problems. Use this Problem Solving Flow Chart. It won't help, but it will distract you from all your worries for a few minutes.

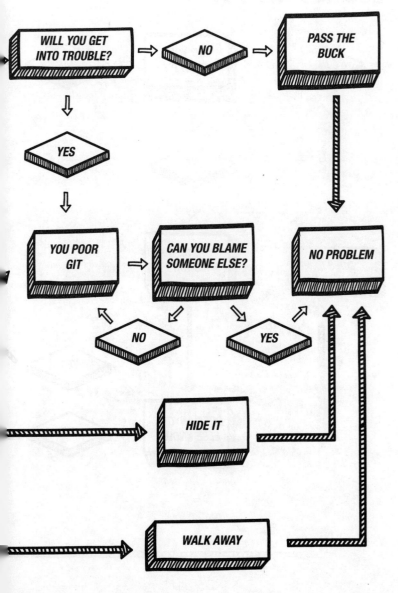

Ferris Bueller's Guide To Life

John Hughes' cult classic, *Ferris Bueller's Day Off*, is the ultimate slacker film about "one man's struggle to take it easy"; a movie that inspires everyone to simply not follow the "rules" for one beautiful day. What would you do with your day off? Where would you go? Let's celebrate Ferris Bueller and rip a page out of his life by taking a well-deceived day off every once in a while. Failing that, get inspired by the eminently quotable teenager:

❝ What is so dangerous about a character like Ferris Bueller is he gives good kids bad ideas. The last thing I need at this point in my career is 1,500 Ferris Bueller disciples running around these halls. He jeopardizes my ability to effectively govern this student body. ❞

Mr Rooney

" Life moves pretty fast. If you don't stop and look around once in a while, you could miss it. "

Ferris Bueller

" The question isn't what are we going to do. The question is what aren't we going to do. "

Ferris Bueller

" A: You can never go too far. B: If I'm gonna get busted, it is not gonna be by a guy like that. "

Ferris Bueller

Office Dares #23 – Six Degrees Of Wikipation

Count how many link clicks it takes to get from one person to another on Wikipedia, in the classic vein of Six Degrees of Separation, the game more popularly known as Kevin Bacon. For example, click from Mary Berry to Adolf Hitler, or from Genghis Khan to Kim Kardashian. The game revolves around carefully clicking the links that appear in each and every article you click through.

This is a great way to waste time with other colleagues. Choose a team of players, pick ten celebrities to get from to the other, make sure you ask everyone to log their links – so you can verify them at the end – and get playing.

Time wasted: 3 hours.

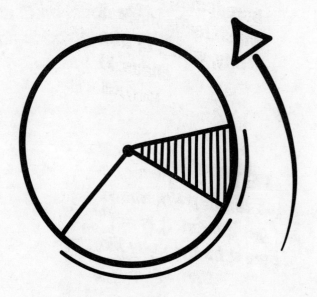

Quote Quota #76

❝ It is only a step from boredom to disillusionment, which leads naturally to self-pity, which in turn ends in chaos. ❞

Manly Hall

*Is Your Job Bullsh*t?*

The obvious answer is clearly yes. But in order to waste a few hours
and to complete your due diligence (which you don't apply in your
day job), take this quiz below, and find out for sure.

1   **Could someone without any qualifications do your job?** ☐

2   **Could your role be carried out if you weren't present in the building?** ☐

3   **Could your work be outsourced to an automated robot of some sort?** ☐

4   **Do you do anything that actually changes your company in any way?** ☐

5   **If yes, do you see those changes on a day-to-day basis?** ☐

6   **If your job wasn't done daily, do you believe that the company would be unable to function?** ☐

7   **Could a monkey, with no experience of language or cognitive function, be able to complete the tasks you do?** ☐

8 Do you attend meetings where the outcome alters the company's working method or profits in any way?

☐

9 Do you feel like you're working towards a realistically achievable goal that will make the world a better place?

☐

10 If your job didn't exist, would anyone think to create it?

☐

11 Did your job exist 50 years ago?

☐

12 Is your company's success dependent on you turning up for work?

☐

13 Do you think a machine would do your job more accurately?

☐

14 Are you currently experiencing redundancies at your workplace and throughout your industry in roles similar to yours?

☐

If you answered every question, congratulations, you wasted some time! Who cares about the answers? Your job is bullsh*t. Take comfort in the fact you knew that anyway.

Office Dares #25 – Go All MacGyver In The Stationery Cupboard

Go into the stationery cupboard. Pick ten items. Take them back to your desk. Now, see if you can make a working engine, or a spaceship, or a fully functional time machine out of the useless bits of crap you found.

Time wasted: 1 hour.

Quote Quota #15

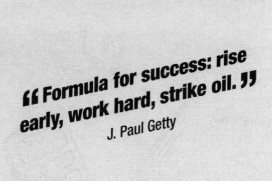

" Formula for success: rise early, work hard, strike oil. "

J. Paul Getty

Office Olympics

Everyone's favourite sporting tournament can be played in an office near you. All you need is the will to shrug off all work responsibilities, the desire to disappoint your boss (if you get caught) and the energy to actually get out of your chair. Oh, and some ping-pong bats.

Top ten games to play at the Office Olympics:

1
Table tennis
The net is the imaginary dividing line between two computer terminals that face each other. Use the palm of your hands as the bats, and that stress ball in your desk drawer as a ball. First to 15 wins.

2
Javelin
Sharpen a pencil. Person who can throw it furthest, wins.

3
Weightlifting
Line up to wrestle the heaviest guy (see above) to the ground first, wins.

4
Wrestling
First to wrestle the heaviest guy (see above) to the ground, wins

5
100m sprint
First to a predetermined spot – roughly 50 metres away – and back, wins.

6
100m hurdles
As above, but just put some office chairs in the runners' way first. Inelegant hurdles, but obstacles nonetheless.

7 **Basketball**
First to throw five scrumpled up memos in a bin from ten metres away, wins.

8 **The Hammer**
Spin your mouse around your head. Whoever throws furthest wins. If you use a wireless mouse... simply move on to the next event.

9 **Luge**
Using a canteen tray, or a sturdy folder, or anything that looks vaguely like a luge: the first person to descend the stairs in one piece is victorious.

10 **Trampoline**
Everyone gets on to their desks, and starts jumping up and down. First person to knock all the items off their desk, wins.

Whoever wins the most events is crowned Office Olympic Champion. The person in second place has to make the winner a cup of tea. Whoever comes last has to photocopy their genitals and send the picture to their mum.

Things That Happen To Everyone In An Office

The following things have happened to us all. This is what offices do to us.

1 You will begin by wearing your best clothes, but will end up not caring at all about what you wear

2 You will develop a caffeine addiction

3 You will develop a crush on a co-worker

4 You will either be freezing or too hot, depending on which part of the office you work in.

5 You will collect the flotsam and jetsam of your entire life in your desk drawer

6 There'll be someone really creepy you'll have to talk to

7 You will bond with someone else over how creepy this person is

8 You'll become really adept at hiding Facebook on your computer

9 You'll hear a co-worker grunting in the bathroom. It'll be awkward

10 You will notice a co-worker doesn't wash their hands after using the bathroom

11 You'll gain weight because of "4pm Biscuit Raids"

12 You will experience weird sexual dreams about people you work with

13 You'll bring your partner to your office and it'll be weird

14 You will get really good at some task, then hate it once everyone starts asking you to help them with it

15 You will form a group of friends that will make it all better

16 You'll develop a relationship known as a work-wife or work-husband

Six Tips To Calling In "Sick" And Getting Away With It

Pulling a sickie can often make you genuinely ill, due to the anxiety and bowel-trembling fear you experience waiting to make that call to your boss. Will they believe you? Here's some handy tips to make sure they do…

1 Make the call at 9.01am – be proactive about it. Don't put it off

2 Don't leave a voicemail – call back every five minutes until you speak to your boss personally

3 Be confident and to the point – don't bumble on for ten minutes apologizing

4 No fake ill sounds and weak coughs – remember you have to go back to work tomorrow, you can't be too ill

5 Ask if there is anything you can do remotely from home, if you "find the strength"

6 Apologize once and only once. Remember you've got nothing to apologize for – you can't help being "ill", right?

Quote Quota #37

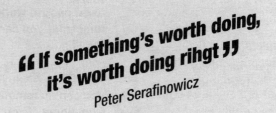

" If something's worth doing, it's worth doing rihgt "

Peter Serafinowicz

Top Ten Excuses _Not_ To Use When Calling In Sick*

*These were genuine excuses some employees gave to their employers in 2012/2013, according to a survey of 1,000 workers and 1,000 employees. Shocking!

1 A can of baked beans landed on my big toe

2 I was swimming too fast and smacked my head on the poolside

3 I've been bitten by an insect

4 My car handbrake broke and it rolled down the hill into a lamppost

5 My dog has had a big fright and I don't want to leave him

6 My hamster died

7 I've injured myself during sex

8 I've had a sleepless night

9 My mum has died (this was the second time the person used this excuse

10 I am hallucinating

11 I am stuck in my house because the door is broken

12 My new girlfriend bit me in a delicate place

13 I burned my hand on the toaster

14 The dog ate my shoes

15 My fish is sick

16 I swallowed white spirit

17 My toe is trapped in the bath tap

18 I'm in A&E, as I got a clothes peg stuck on my tongue

19 I drank too much and fell asleep on some-one's floor – I don't know where I am

20 My trousers split on the way to work

Top Ten Most Believable Excuses When Calling In Sick

If you want your boss to believe your sickie pleas, then stick with one of these guaranteed* believable excuses:

1 I've got the norovirus (use between November and April)

2 I've got abdominal pains (use only if you're female)

3 My car was broken into this morning

4 I've got food poisoning

5 My girlfriend's great-great-grandmother just died – she's devastated.

6 I've locked myself in between the hallway and the front door

7 My house has been burgled. (I used this once, after actually being burgled the night before. I'm sure my boss always thought it was an excuse, though!)

8 My cat needs to go to the vet to be put down

9 My dog isn't breathing – I can't leave it alone

10 I developed a rash on my groin that needs checking out

*In no way a guarantee.

Quote Quota #45

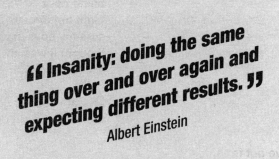

❝ Insanity: doing the same thing over and over again and expecting different results. ❞

Albert Einstein

Words To Make You Sound Clever

Drop these smart bombs into conversations, and your boss may just *not* look at you with contempt today. Not a guarantee.

1   **Byzantine**   Highly involved or intricate

2   **Capricious**   Impulsive and unpredictable

3   **Dilettante**   Showing frivolous or superficial interest

4   **Equanimity**   Steadiness of mind under stress

5   **Fastidious**   Difficult to please

6   **Finagle**   To trick, swindle or cheat

7   **Machiavellian**   Unprincipled and crafty

8 **Philistine**   A person who is uninterested in intellectual pursuits

9 **Quid pro quo**   This for that

10 **Sycophant**   A self-serving flatterer, a brownnoser

11 **Ubiquitous**   Being present everywhere at once

12 **Zealous**   Enthusiastic; fervent; fanatical

13 **Boondoggle**   Work of little or no value done merely to look busy

14 **Malinger**   To evade responsibility by pretending to be ill

Office Jargon To Keep An Eye On

Here's a quick guide to some of the more confusing corporate lingo that most of your co-workers – in particular, middle managers – will use most of the time without any care or consideration for its etymology or meaning.

1 **Not Enough Bandwidth**
Example: "Sorry, Steve, I'm don't have enough bandwidth for that."

2 **Idea shower**
Example: "Let's meet today at 2pm and idea shower this project, yeah?"

3 **Radar**
Example: "It's been hectic – but you're on my radar now."

4 **Thinking forward**
Example: "Thinking forward, what's our strategy?"

5 **360 degree thinking**
Example: "Let's 360 degree think this, team."

6 **At the end of the day**
Example: "At the end of the day, it's got to get done."

7 **Version 2.0**
Example: "This'll be version 2.0 – better than the original"

8 **Al Desco**
Example: "I forgot to have breakfast this morning... so I had it Al Desco."

9 **Heads-up**
Example: "Just a quick heads-up, numbers are down."

10 **Downsizing**
Example: "We're downsizing and you've been downsized the most."

The Honest Truth

Seventy-five per cent of all office minions believe they can run the company better than the management. 100% of them are right.

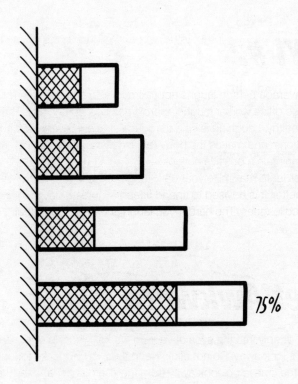

75%

FYI #1

A tiny 2 per cent drop in body water can cause difficulty focusing on your computer screen, short-term memory loss and trouble working out the solutions to basic problems. So, remember to hydrate every 30 minutes. FYI – the less interesting pages in this book were all written when I was dehydrated, OK.

FYI #2

The average person laughs approximately 13 times a day. The aveage office worker laughs approximately 0.3 times day. That's not healthy. Laughing is said to reduce stress, prevent pain and infections, and makes the body release endorphins that can help you maintain a positive outlook.

In order to maximize your daily laugh count, and make yourself feel better, it is advised to spend fifteen minutes a day laughing at your colleagues. The harder you laugh, the better you'll feel.

Get Awkward #1

Stare deeply into the eyes of your co-worker who sits opposite you. Do not look away. Do not blink. Keep them in your gaze for one hour. After the time is up, look away from them in disgust and tell them that they're "dead inside".

It's A Dirty Job But Someone's Got To Do It...

Working in an office is so dreadful that 8 out of ten people still would prefer to work at the jobs below than work inside an office.

1 Portable Toilet Cleaner

2 Sewage Treatment Workers

3 Toilet Attendant

4 Nude Model

5 Embalmer

6 Roadkill Collector

7 Castrato

8 Poultry Kill Room Attendant

9 Animal Masturbator

10 Pet Food Taster

11 Sewer Inspector

12 Baby Chicken Sexer

Piles Of Work

There are lots of strains and pressures we put on our body during our average week at the office. Not least on our poor behinds, which get sat on for hours on end with little exercise in between. Below is a list of famous people who suffered from piles – perhaps they also spent too much time on the loo, hiding from work and their bosses.

1. **Alfred the Great**
2. **Napoleon Bonaparte**
3. **Ernest Hemingway**
4. **Marilyn Monroe**
5. **Karl Marx**
6. **Elizabeth Taylor**

Get Awkward #2

Grab your boss' hand on your walk to the next staff meeting. If they try to let go – which they will – simply tell them, "Sorry, I must have misread the situation," before mouthing the words "I love you" to them as they walk into the meeting room. This will completely discombobulate them for the entire meeting.

FYI #3

The average commute to work, in the UK, takes 45 minutes and the average distance travelled is approximately 8½ miles. That's at least a 16-mile round trip every day. However, recent studies show that office fingers will travel 2.6 miles across the keyboard every single day!

Me Time

Spending time in cramped workspaces, cubicles and "desk stations" with people we resent and ridicule is tough work. Every now and then you need a little ME TIME in the office, which isn't just sat down on the loo watching Netflix and occasionally flushing to let people know you haven't disappeared down the hole. Here are some great ways to enjoy some quality ME TIME at work:

1 **Book a Meeting Room** – and then just hide there for hours pretending to work.

2 **Walk "to the Post Office"** – pretend you have something important to send.

3 **Listen to a "work-related podcast" on your iPhone** – it's actually Beyoncé's latest album.

4 **Watch a "TED Talk" with your headphones in** – no one will realize it has nothing to do with your job.

5 **Make a tea round** – for the whole office. Gets you away from your desk for a good 20 minutes.

Up In Your Business

The average person – that's you – spends 100,000 hours of their 650,000 hours alive on earth life pursuing a career. if you work in an office, that's 100,000 hours of smelling other people's farts and BO.

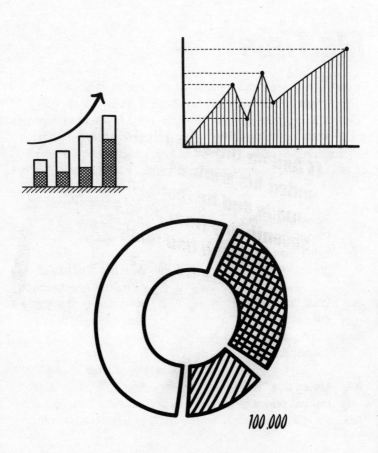

100,000

Quote Quota #21

" And on the seventh day God ended his work which he had made and he rested on the seventh day from all his work which he had made. "

Genesis II, Verse II

Famous People Who Lost Their Jobs Before They Were Famous

Lord Sugar is famous for pointing at hapless individuals and telling them, "You're Fired", to the nation's squeals of delight. But, in truth, getting fired is one of the most embarrassing things that can happen to an office worker. Thankfully, job loss has happened to these wonderful people too...

1 Walt Disney (he "lacked imagination and had no good ideas")

2 J.K. Rowling (got the boot as a secretary from Amnesty International)

3 Anna Wintour ("I recommend that you all get fired," she said after)

4 Madonna (she was let go on her first day after squirting jelly on her customers)

5 Oprah Winfrey (as a news anchor for Baltimore's WJZ-TV)

6 Robert Redford (was found asleep on the job!)

7 Thomas Edison (spilled acid on the floor of a laboratory)

8 Steve Jobs (fired from Apple, the company he created)

9 Michael Jordan (was cut from his high school basketball team!)

10 Rudyard Kipling ("You just don't know how to use the English language," his newspaper editor told him)

Top Ten Ways To Avoid Fixing A Printer Jam

All sorts of things go wrong in an office – on a daily basis. But when a printer breaks down, so does the humanity of your colleagues. Here's how to avoid doing what they won't.

1. **Pretend to go to a meeting – let someone else notice and fix it.**
2.
3.
4.
5.
6.
7.
8.
9.
10. **Hopefully by now, it's fixed.**

PRINTER JAM RULES
If it's broke, don't try to fix it.
If you broke it, don't try to fix it.
If someone else broke it, let everyone know you didn't break it.

110%

Are you always told to "do more" at work? Do you always give 110 per cent? No?

Well, here's our guaranteed guide to always giving 110 per cent at work. If anyone ever doubts your work ethic – and they should – throw these percentages about how hard you work back in their face.

Monday 30 per cent
Tuesday 30 per cent
Wednesday 25 per cent
Thursday 23 per cent
Friday 2 per cent

Total = 110 per cent

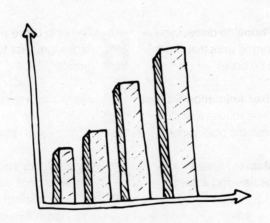

Mr Jobs

You can't have a book about office jobs and not talk about the man whose inventions have saved us all from actually doing our job – the late, great Steve Jobs (1955–2011). Thanks to this man's efforts, we now have the weapons of mass distraction to help us achieve less at work as well as stop us from getting bored. His achievements can be listed quite simply – just randomly put an "i" in front of any word and you'll probably name many of Apple's bestselling products. But here are definitely ten of his best creations, in no particular order.

1 **Apple Music** (great to listen to drown out colleagues voices)

2 **Apple Music Festival** (a place to go to that isn't work)

3 **iPhone** (to distract you from all work that needs to be done)

4 **Pixar Animation Studios** (great movies to watch when the boss is out)

5 **iMac** (beats using a fax)

6 **iPad** (pocket-sized – perfect for hiding on your desk)

7 **iPod** (once a great way to smuggle music into work hours)

8 **The App Store** (Angry Birds – great for toilet breaks)

9 **Apple Store** (a great place to work, should you be made redundant)

10 **Bringing back black polo neck jumpers into fashion** (they've always suited you)

Top Ten: How To Get Ahead In Business

Work may be nine hours of boredom punctuated by a few random minutes of fear, anxiety and panic, but for those of you who actually want to succeed at work (without really trying), then this list below is guaranteed to help you along the way:

1 **Always leave one minute after the boss has gone, never before**

2 **Make sure your tea mug is the mug with the company logo on**

3 **Decorate your workspace with motivational signs and quotations; print off new quotations every week and place them near your monitor**

4 **Routinely send round all-staff emails alerting colleagues to sponsor your most recent charity crowd-funding event**

5 **Always walk round the office holding folders, and always look as if you're in a rush to get to wherever it is you're going – even if it's just the toilet**

6 Every time you see your boss, compliment them on their hair, clothes or appearance. Drip-fed flattery goes a long way

7 Bring in baked treats, chocolates and sweets at least twice a week

8 Never call in sick: it's better to fake an illness and then be sent home rather than have colleagues question your illness when you're not there

9 Keep a journal of every unflattering or gossipy utterance that a co-worker says about another co-worker, or every time your boss does something fraudulent or illegal in terms of company policy. This journal might one day save your life

10 Develop really unreadable handwriting and then appear to take copious amounts of "important" notes in every meeting you ever attend. Even if you're just scribbling down the word "tits" over and over again, co-workers will think you're being attentive and officious

Inbox Full

It is estimated that 144.8 billion emails are sent ever single day. That's around 20 emails per person for every man, woman and child on earth! 65 per cent of all those emails sent are spam and 30 per cent of all your emails sent during working hours are personal. The average office worker spends 36 days a year answering work emails. Office workers in London, in particular, receive close to 9,000 emails each year – roughly 25 emails a day.

Playlist – Songs To Calm You Down

Stressful meeting? Frustrating appraisal? We feel your pain. This playlist will help lower your blood pressure...

- ▶ 1.   Queen – Don't Stop Me Now
- ▶ 2.   Fleetwood Mac – Go Your Own Way
- ▶ 3.   Snow Patrol – Chasing Cars
- ▶ 4.   The Black Eyed Peas – Let's Get It Started
- ▶ 5.   Coldplay – Paradise
- ▶ 6.   Lily Allen – Smile
- ▶ 7.   Prince – Purple Rain
- ▶ 8.   Tracy Chapman – Fast Car
- ▶ 9.   Calvin Harris – Ready for the Weekend
- ▶ 10. George Ezra – Budapest

Buzzword Bingo!

The office-based disease currently spreading itself like Avian Flu across the globe goes by a few nasty-sounding nouns – Jargon, Buzzwords, Cliché, Waffle, and so on. In your office, you'll know it by it's true name: bullsh*t. The only cure for this utterly depressing infection is Buzzword Bingo!, a Bingo-style quiz where frustrated office workers (just like you) prepare Bingo cards with corporate buzzwords on them and tick them off when they are spoken during an office-related event, such as a pointless sales call, boring monthly staff meeting or your dreaded one-to-one weekly "catchup" meetings with the boss. The goal is to tick off as many buzzwords as possible and and then yell "Bullsh*t!" as loud as possible. If you haven't worked it out already, the whole point of this game is to let your entire office know when someone in your office is talking complete and utter bullsh*t.

Here's a practice Buzzword Bingo card for you to photocopy and go nuts with:

⭐ •B I N G O•

BANDWIDTH	THINKING FORWARD	BLUE SKY THINKING	VERSION 2.0	TRENDING
HEADS-UP	ACTION	JUDGEMENT CALL	CHECK IN THE BOX	AIR IT OUT
DOWNSIZING	RECRUITING	◯	DROP THE BALL	BRAINSTORM
RISK MANAGEMENT	OUT OF THE LOOP	TOUCH BASE	PROACTIVE	STRATEGY
UNIQUE SELLING PROPOSITION	KEY PERFORMANCE INDICATORS	END-USER PERSPECTIVE	GAME CHANGER	TEAM WORK

Quote Quota #12

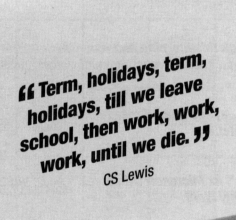

" Term, holidays, term, holidays, till we leave school, then work, work, work, until we die. "

CS Lewis

Office Puns
(We Love To Hate)

Try and sneak these crafty little puns into conversation, if only to make yourself laugh. Watch your co-workers' eyes roll with pain every time you whip them out:

To the Cleaner…
Did you hear about the new broom that just came out? It's sweeping the nation.

To A Co-Worker
I ate a clock this morning and thought that was time consuming… but that meeting went on for hours.

To A Minion
I just ate way too much Greek food for lunch. Now I falafel.

To the IT Manager
If you don't fix Microsoft Office, you'll be in big trouble. You have my Word.

To your Boss
I'm so committed to my job that I only eat office supplies. It's a staple diet.

To A Co-Worker
Everyone's off work at the moment sick. It must be a staff infection.

First Jobs Of The Rich And Famous: Top 10 – Part 2

Celebrities are just like us. They too have suffered the embarrassment of having to work for a living. The only difference is, they are universally adored for getting paid to do nothing and the absolute inverse is applicable to the rest of us.

1. **Channing Tatum – Stripper**
2. **Whoppi Goldberg – Morgue beautician**
3. **Hugh Jackman – PE teacher**
4. **Jennifer Aniston – Telemarketer**
5. **Harrison Ford – Carpenter**
6. **Vince Vaughn – Lifeguard**
7. **George Clooney – Door-to-door insurance salesman**
8. **Nicole Kidman – Massage therapist**
9. **Christopher Walken – Lion tamer**
10. **Sylvester Stallone – Lion-cage cleaner**

Quote Quota #55

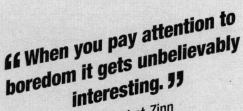

"When you pay attention to boredom it gets unbelievably interesting."

Jon Kabat-Zinn

Drawing A Blank

Focus all your boredom onto the blank square below. Don't stop until you feel all of the day's pointlessness and frustration running towards the exit door in your brain. Once you've finished, shake the book vigorously to waft away the negative energy you have absorbed throughout the day.

LOOK HERE!

The Never-To-Say And Never-To-Do List

Your bosses will spend much of their time wanting you to do what they say, but will never actually want you to say what they do. Because most of what they say is utter rubbish. Keep an ear out for these braincell-killing words of wisdom today….

1. **Push the envelope**

2. **Enjoy a thought shower**

3. **Kick the can around the garage**

4. **Press play on an idea**

5. **Brain storm**

6. **Make a reality sandwich**

7. **High-five a colleague after an excellent PowerPoint presentation**

8. **Ideagasm**

9. **Synergize**

10. **Trend upwards**

REMEMBER

Every time you hear these phrases, you lose 300 brain cells. How many more can you stand to lose?

Office Photocopier Rules

If the photocopier toner needs replacing or a paper jam occurs while you're using it, and to ensure the ongoing inefficient running of the office, please carry out the follow instructions:

1. **Walk away**
2. **Whistle a jaunty tune**
3. **Take an early lunch**

Get Awkward #3

Say the words "I love you" at the end of every conversation today.

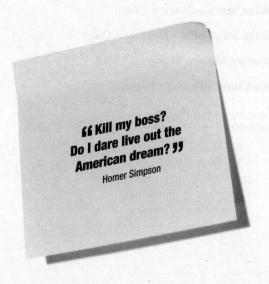

“Kill my boss? Do I dare live out the American dream?”
Homer Simpson

Playlist – Songs To Get You Pumped Up To Ask For A Raise

Money makes the office go round, but yet the buck stops literally just before knocking at your door. Go figure. Pump yourself up into a frenzy and walk straight into your boss's office and don't take no for answer.

▶ 1.   **Money For Nothing – Dire Straits**

▶ 2.   **Working Day and Night – Michael Jackson**

▶ 3.   **Take the Money and Run – The Steve Miller Band**

▶ 4.   **Slave To The Wage – Placebo**

▶ 5.   **I Need A Dollar – Aloe Blacc**

▶ 6.   **After Taxes – Johnny Cash**

▶ 7.   **Bills, Bills, Bills – Destiny's Child**

▶ 8.   **Money, Money, Money – ABBA**

▶ 9.   **Ka-Ching! – Shania Twain**

▶ 10. **Money – Pink Floyd**

Quote Quota #33

" Often, people work long hard hours at jobs they hate, to earn money to buy things they don't need, to impress people they don't like. "

Nigel Marsh

Post-it Note Prank

This is an oldie, but a goldie, and a prank that will provide a definite flash of colour and excitement to your dull, cold and lifeless working environment.

First things first: go to the stationery cupboard. I assume you know where this is. Pick up a six-pack of the large, squared Post-it notes. Any colour will suffice.

Next time your office nemesis – or just any old random work person who you can't stand the sight of – goes for lunch, quickly cover every square inch of their desk area with Post-its. Do not leave a space un-noted. Cover as much surface area as you can; there are 100 notes per pad, so you should be able to use up 600 Post-it notes without much effort. If you're worried about wasting good quality office supplies, then feel free to print out a whole ream of paper with pictures of David Hasselhoff in just his red *Baywatch* shorts instead, and decorate your victim's "working space" with more Hasselhoff chest hair than any one person should see in a lifetime.

[Top Tip]

Pick your victim wisely. Don't choose your boss, or anyone who will rat on you and get you fired. Choose someone who you know will get pissed off at first ... but then laugh it off. At the end of the day you both want to be laughing at how much office time and work energy was wasted on seeing the prank through to its extreme conclusion.

Top Ten: Stressbusters

Forgot those squidgy little balls you crush between your palms. That's too easy. When you really need to bust some serious stress, try the following:

1 Try breaking a plastic 30cm ruler in half with your head (it's impossible)

2 Open up a Microsoft Word.doc and type as many different swear words as possible. Don't stop until you've drawn a complete blank. By then, your stress will have drained totally from your being and you will have gained a massive insight into your own devious psyche

3 Smell fresh coffee. This cheers everyone up

4 Rip a whole ream of A4 paper in half – good luck!

5 Google "Cat strokes pig" and watch the video that appears on repeat

6 Squirt a lemon in your eye or rub chilli in your eye – the pain will distract you from the stress

7 Staple your two perlicules together (Google what they are first)

8 Wrap a whole dispenser of sellotape around your head and then slowly untangle it – the pain will distract you from the stress

9 Edit a Wikipedia page

10 Write a list of everyone you've slept with – not in chronological order, but alphabetical

Things We'd All Like To Say To Our Boss

Most of us usually think of the perfect response to our manager's inane questions only after they've stormed out of the room. Have these lines prepared in advance and you'll always get the first and last word in…

"Of course I don't look busy. I did it right the first time."

"You've changed your mind? Well, there's a surprise."

"No, I'm not busy – feel free to waste my time."

"Would you like to offer to make me a cup of tea for once?"

"I'll stay late – if you do."

"The best part of my day is when you've stopped telling me how to do your job and concentrate on yours."

"You don't be mad to work here … but you definitely fulfil that criteria."

"I'm sorry I'm late, but I'd thought I'd be a bit more like you today."

"Good morning… well, it was before you arrived."

"Don't have a good night."

Quote Quota #91

> **" The brain is a wonderful organ. It starts working the moment you get up in the morning, and does not stop until you get into the office. "**
>
> Robert Frost

Office Monkeys

This is an old office joke, one you've probably heard a million times, but it's worth repeating because it accurately describes every office.

"An office is like a tree full of monkeys, all on different branches at different levels. The monkeys on top look down and see a tree full of smiling faces. The monkeys on the bottom look up and see nothing but arseholes."

Get Awkward #4

Send a picture of a can of Spam attached to an All Staff email. Then follow-up that email with an apology for the spam email.

Untitled Folder Roulette

A good way to kill some time in your working day is to create 50 folders on your desktop all labeled "untitled folder". Dump all your work in different folders and then every morning guess what folder that day's work is in. At the end of each day, move the folders about. This will kill many hours mindlessly.

Create Your Own: Spinning Rainbow Wheel Of Death

The Spinning Rainbow Wheel of Death – a sure sign that you're about to lose all the unsaved work you've been working on for the past three hours – is one of the most annoying aspects of working with a computer. However, let's turn this object of doom into a object of fun – and create your own multicoloured paper pinwheel.

You will need:
A4 paper, a picture nail, a straw, colouring pens

1. Draw a large circle on an A4 piece of paper.
2. Colour in the circle all the colours of the rainbow
3. Cut the circle out
4. Pierce the centre of the circle with a picture naill
5. Pierce the top of a straw with the nail

Now, every time someone in the office asks you a stupid question, blow on your rainbow wheel until they go away.

Playlist – Songs To Sing During A Bad Day

So, you've had a bad day? Wallow in it with these tunes that'll make it worse, and therefore make it a lot better...

- ▶ 1. **Nowhere Man – The Beatles**
- ▶ 2. **I've Had It – Black Flag**
- ▶ 3. **Lose Yourself – Eminem**
- ▶ 4. **Get Over it – OK Go**
- ▶ 5. **Happy Hour – Palladium**
- ▶ 6. **Comfortably Numb – Pink Floyd**
- ▶ 7. **There There – Radiohead**
- ▶ 8. **(I Can't Get No) Satisfaction – The Rolling Stones**
- ▶ 9. **Don't Stand So Close To Me – The Police**
- ▶ 10. **The Underdog – Spoon**

Don't Walk, Snudge

Did you know there is an actual word to describe striding around the office trying to look terribly busy, when in fact you're doing nothing at all (except killing time). It's called snudging, from the verb to snudge. Give it a whirl – it might be the only thing that impresses your boss today!

Get Awkward #5

Place a segment of orange in the bottom of your mouth, *a la* Marlon Brando in *The Godfather*. Then send an email to your co-workers with the subject line: "An Offer You Can't Refuse". Anyone who comes to your desk to enquire what on earth you mean, tell them that you'll do whatever they ask of you for the rest of the day, while speaking in a heavy Italian-American accent like Don Corleone.

Dream Job

In October 2015, a survey from the *Independent* newspaper threw a spotlight on Britain's Ten Dream Jobs. Surprise, surprise! Not one of them is office-based. In fact, judging by the list, the entire country would rather be *absolutely anywhere else* than sitting at their desk in an office.

1. **Footballer**
2. **Private Detective**
3. **Actor**
4. **Spy**
5. **Becoming My Own Boss**
6. **Singer**
7. **Vet**
8. **Astronaut**
9. **Dancer**
10. **Mad Scientist**

Quote Quota #25

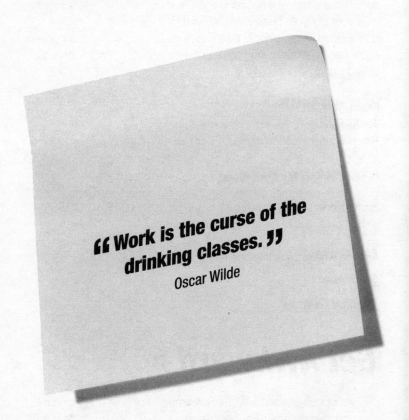

❝ Work is the curse of the drinking classes. ❞

Oscar Wilde

I Love My Boss

Nobody likes a kiss-ass. Nobody likes a smart-ass. Certianly, no-body likes a smart kiss-ass. But if you want to get ahead in office-dom these days, why not send this email below. Your colleagues will hate you, but your boss will LOVE you.

In a world where people take notice of the slogan on your coffee cup – as if it defines who you are – why not just turn the flattery dial upto 11 and be done with it...

From: You
To: All Staff
Re: Has anyone seen my I LOVE MY BOSS mug?

Apologies for the all-staffer,

Has anyone seen my mug? It has the words "I LOVE MY BOSS" written on it. It is of great importance to me.

Anyone who returns this cherished item will receive £5.

Thanks!

Get Awkward #6

Buy your boss a World's Worst Boss mug from Amazon. Hand it to them on their birthday. For best results, fill it with freshly milked urine.

Christmas Party Ingredients

Most office Christmas parties are a recipe for disaster. Here are all the ingredients you need to make this year's party as "unforgettable" as last year's:

Two office hunks
Three drunken chairman
Four accounting birds
No wedding rings
Six CEOs flirting
Seven interns crying
Eight empty stomachs
Nine sales assistants dancing
Ten salesman ogling
Eleven people puking
Twelve Uber bookings
and
A trip to the local A&E

Playlist – Songs To Start An Office Revolution

Revolt! Revolt! Turn these songs up loud now!

- ▶ 1. **Packt Like Sardines In A Crushd Tin Box – Radiohead**
- ▶ 2. **Bye Bye Bad Man – The Stone Roses**
- ▶ 3. **Everybody Wants To Rule The World – Tears For Fears**
- ▶ 4. **World Of Our Own – Westlife**
- ▶ 5. **I Want To Break Free – Queen**
- ▶ 6. **Revolution Song – Noel Gallagher**
- ▶ 7. **The Boy In the Bubble – Paul Simon**
- ▶ 8. **Drag Me Down – One Direction**
- ▶ 9. **Killing In The Name – Rage Against the Machine**
- ▶ 10. **I Hate My Job – Cam'ron**

Quote Quota #40

"It is impossible to enjoy idling thoroughly unless one has plenty of work to do."
Jerome K Jerome

Working Day Breakdown

We constantly moan to our co-workers how much work we have on but, let's be honest, no matter how busy we claim to be, we still spend most of day trying hard not to work. Like so:

09:00–09:15	Arrival time
09:15–09:45	Breakfast
09:45–10:00	Toilet
10:15–11:00	Check your inbox, reply to personal emails
11:00–11:30	Make your round of tea; cruise the office to see what people are doing for lunch
11:30–12:00	Check Facebook/Twitter/Instagram
12:00–12:30	Prepare for lunch
12:30–13:45	Lunch
13:45–14:00	Toilet
14:00–14:15	Make another round of tea
14:15–15.30	A pointless meeting
15:30–16:00	Confirm plans for the evening with friends/partner/family
16:00–16:45	General web browsing
16:45–17:15	Urgently cram in all the work for the day
17:15–17:25	Prepare to go home
17:28	Go home

Total work time: 2.5 hours
Total time wasted: 5.5 hours

Germ-Infected Disease Holes

The average office toilet has 49 germs per square inch. Your office computer keyboard has, on average, 4,000 germs per square inch. But that's nothing compared to your office phone – it has 25,000 germs per square inch. Remember that, next time your too lazy to walk to your boss's office. A virus, such as norovirus, the common cold or stomach flu, can travel around an office in four hours.

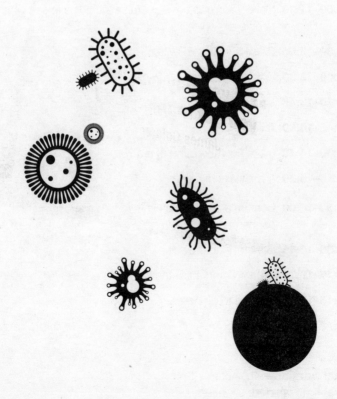

Quote Quota #24

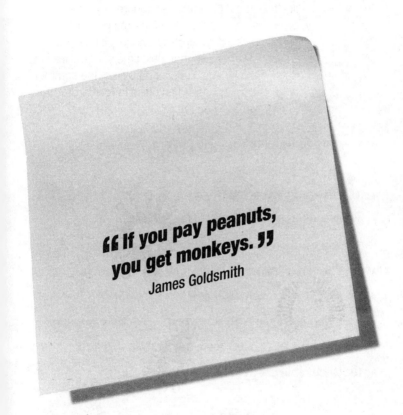

❝ If you pay peanuts, you get monkeys. ❞
James Goldsmith

Playlist – Songs To Sit And Daydream The Day Away With

When it all gets a bit much on a Friday afternoon, curl up into the foetal position under your desk, pop in your headphones, and daydream the rest of the day away with these songs guaranteed to make you forget where you are…

▸ 1. **Only To Be With You – Roachford**

▸ 2. **Relax – Frankie Goes To Hollywood**

▸ 3. **Lay, Lady, Lay – Bob Dylan**

▸ 4. **Sunshine Of Your Love – Ella Fitzgerald**

▸ 5. **You've Lost That Lovin' Feeling – The Righteous Brothers**

▸ 6. **The Power Of Love – Huey Lewis & The News**

▸ 7. **I Want To Know What Love Is – Foreigner**

▸ 8. **I Wanna Dance With Somebody – Whitney Houston**

▸ 9. **Because You Loved Me – Céline Dion**

▸ 10. **Cheeseburger In Paradise – Jimmy Buffett**

The Way To Avoid Making A Tea Round

Pretend to go to a meeting, but say out loud, "If anyone makes a cup of tea while I'm gone, my mug is on my desk. Milk, no sugar please!" and then walk out. Pop back after ten minutes. By doing this, you'll have whetted the appetite of your colleagues for tea; by suggesting the office was devoid of tea, someone will immediately fill it with tea. Like space, offices hate a vacuum.

Office Dare #247

Find a copy of the Telephone List on the company's Admin server. This is the list that details every worker's telephone extension. Change all the numbers around. Then send the revised form around on an All Staff email from the Reception computer, or whoever usually sends those things around, when no-one is looking. Then laugh hysterically when your boss is inundated with a million calls meant for the IT department.

Quote Quota #62

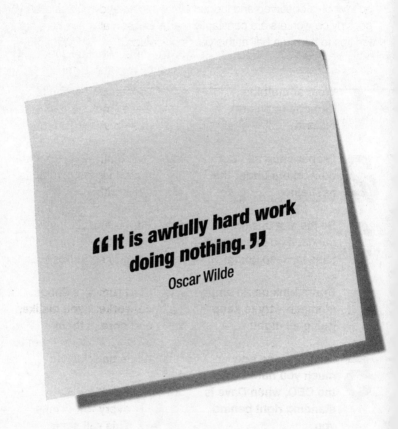

❝ It is awfully hard work doing nothing. ❞

Oscar Wilde

Office Party Rules

We often forget these days that even though office Christmas parties or outings are parties, they are still business events where our behaviour is observed and judged every minute and impressions by gossipy co-workers are constantly made. But sod all that – here are ten tips to having a ball at this year's office do:

1 Wear something raunchy (men and women)

2 Proper snog all your co-workers under the mistletoe

3 Be the first to start the conga. If no one else joins in, keep going

4 Don't drink on an empty stomach – try to keep going all night!

5 Tell everyone how much you hate Dave, the CEO, when Dave is standing right behind you

6 Be the last person to leave – no one can gossip about you then

7 Wait until someone you fancy is leaving, jump in a taxi with them

8 Be the first on the dancefloor. Even if there is no dancefloor

9 Start rumours about co-workers you dislike, and spread them around. Wait for them to come back to you

10 Vomit tactically every few drinks. This will save it erupting out spontaneously all down your clothes

The Five Rules Of A Smooth Running Office

This is an old office joke that your dad no doubt used in the 1970s. Nonetheless, it's a joke that is as timely today as it ever was…

1 **All targets met**

2 **All customers satisfied**

3 **All systems fully operational**

4 **All staff keen and well motivated**

5 **All pigs fed and ready to fly**

Morning Motivation Playlist

These songs will get you fired up and raring to go in the morning:

- ▶ **Don't Give Up – Peter Gabriel (feat. Kate Bush)**
- ▶ **Brother, Can You Spare A Dime? – Bing Crosby**
- ▶ **Taking Care Of Business – Bachman-Turner Overdrive**
- ▶ **Work To Do – The Isley Brothers**
- ▶ **Whistle While You Work – The Seven Dwarfs**
- ▶ **Heigh-Ho – Seven Dwarfs**
- ▶ **Money – Pink Floyd**
- ▶ **The Promised Land – Bruce Springsteen**
- ▶ **Don't Stop Believin' – Journey**
- ▶ **Eye of the Tiger – Survivor**
- ▶ **Sweet Home Alabama – Lynyrd Skynyrd**
- ▶ **Beat It – Michael Jackson**
- ▶ **Don't Stop Me Now – Queen**
- ▶ **Lose Yourself – Eminem**
- ▶ **Firework – Katy Perry**
- ▶ **Rock You Like a Hurricane – Scorpions**
- ▶ **Run the World (Girls) – Beyoncé**
- ▶ **Just Got Paid – Johnny Kemp**
- ▶ **Nice Work If You Can Get It – George and Ira Gershwin**
- ▶ **There's No Business Like Show Business – Irving Berlin**
- ▶ **My Old Man's A Dustman – Lonnie Donegan**

Quote Quota #45

❝ Never do today that which will become someone else's responsibility tomorrow. ❞

Anon

One In Four

One in four office workers are unhappy with their job – with men, aged between 21–35, working in IT most likely to be the unhappiest – according to the 2015 Happiness at Work survey. Put your hand up if you are that unlucky one?

Office Dare #99

Log on to one of your co-workers' computers. In the drop down menu in the Settings folder, find the Macro tab. In this setting instruct the computer to change all mentions of the person's name – let's call them "Ian" – to the word "douche". Everytime that person types their name in an email, or a wordprocessor file, the word immediately changes to "douche."

Quote Quota #78

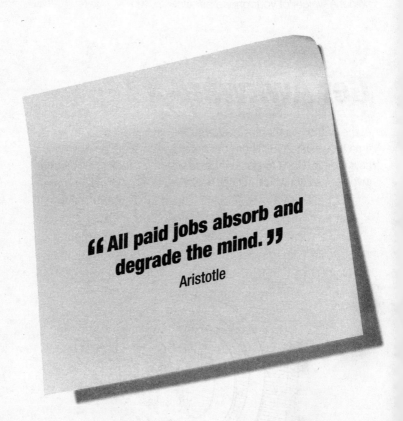

"All paid jobs absorb and degrade the mind."
Aristotle

Office Hack

Want to make your own phone stand? No problem, grab a large paperclip and bend it around into the shape of a stand – the clip will hold the weight of your phone perfectly.

Get Awkward #7

At the end of the month, invoice your boss for the amount of your time they wasted. Bill them per hour, and demand payment within seven days. Don't forget to include the time it took to create the invoice – an act which in itself was a waste of your time.

Quote Quota #47

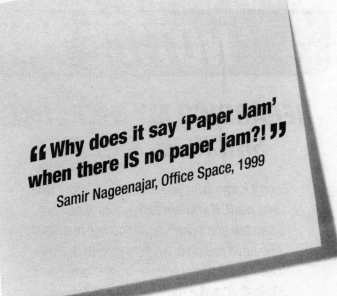

**" Why does it say 'Paper Jam'
when there IS no paper jam?! "**

Samir Nageenajar, Office Space, 1999

Office Fridge Threat

In order to keep your lunch safe from the vultures that circle your lunch, sellotape this sign – the infamous 'I Will Kill You' passage taken from the film *Taken*, to the front of the fridge as a warning to all:

NOTICE

REGARDING MY DIET COKE, SNICKERS AND BLT

I don't know who you are. I don't know what you want. If you are looking for a ransom, I can tell you I don't have money, but what I do have are a very particular set of skills. Skills I have acquired over a very long career. Skills that make me a nightmare for people like you. If you don't eat my food, that'll be the end of it. I will not look for you, I will not pursue you. But if you eat my snickers, I will look for you, I will find you and I will make you disappear.

How To Avoid Going To A Meeting

Meetings go on and on, don't they? Try these smart and blame-free techniques to get out of meetings now!

1 Simply don't go to begin with. What's the worst that could happen?

2 Don't go – but tell people you were sitting in Meeting Room B, for hours, waiting for people to turn up.

3 Get your mother, friend, or partner to call precisely five minutes into the meeting, and then dash out urgently, as if it's an important life-or-death call.

4 Ask the receptionist to come and get you as soon as the meeting starts because, "there's someone important-looking waiting for you in reception."

5 Tell colleagues that you'll conference call into the meeting, but then start doing crackly and static noises with your mouth and blame the "infernal technology" for not working.

6 Download a Fire Alarm Siren ringtone on your phone, and just as the meeting starts, phone yourself – everyone will think the fire alarm is going off.

7 Start a rumour that you saw a rat in the meeting room, as everyone sits down. Rattle paper under the desk, and shout "There it is!", and jump on your chair.

8 Walk into the meeting very late, but bring biscuits. Everyone will forget that you were late.

9 Create confusion before the meeting starts about whether the meeting is going ahead or not. Then when it does, you can argue legitimately that you thought it wasn't.

10 Sellotape a fresh piece of fish behind the radiator, an hour before the meeting starts. When everyone sits down to start, the stench will be unbearable.

Quote Quota #82

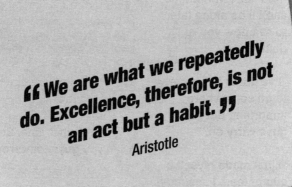

" We are what we repeatedly do. Excellence, therefore, is not an act but a habit. "

Aristotle

Curb Your Enthusiasm

One way bosses and senior managers seem to get ahead in the workplace is by curbing their enthusiasm to do the work that is offered to them. Here are ten phrases senior staff and managers use on a daily basis, to wriggle out of being decent human beings:

1 "I'm too busy to do that now. It will have to wait. Unless you can do it?"

2 "You start without me, and I'll be along later to see how you're doing."

3 "I've got to leave early to go somewhere important, but you guys carry on."

4 "I just made myself a cup of tea... I assumed you guys were OK without one."

5 "I wasn't involved in this project until it was a success, and now it has everything to do with me."

6 "This project was a success last time I looked at it."

7 "Don't worry, I'll step in and save the day."

8 "At the end of the day, someone is to blame. And that someone isn't me."

9 "It's lunchtime. See you guys tomorrow."

10 "Have a relaxing weekend. Don't forget I need those reports on Monday morning first thing."

Things That Will Make You Cry Today

Eighty per cent of all office workers feel stressed about their jobs, and only 30 per cent feel inspired and engaged about their own careers. These are the root causes of those problems. Which one – if not all – will you encounter today?

1. **Micromanagement**

2. **Lack of career progression and/or promotion**

3. **Job insecurity**

4. **No confidence in management leadership**

5. **Lack of recognition for outstanding work performance**

6. **Poor communication**

7. **Arsehole co-workers**

8. **Boredom**

9. **Deleting an important file; and having to start over**

10. **"A freeze on all salaries for the foreseeable future"**

Office Acronym

What does it all mean? Is there hidden meaning in the word "office"?

Only
Fools
Find
Idiotic
Colleagues
Entertaining

I admit, it's a fairly crap acronym – but can you think
of a better one?

Have a go below...

O
F
F
I
C
E

Sense Of Perspective

Perspective is often one of the first things in offices that get jettisoned out of the window when people are overworked. Employees in offices love getting their knickers in a twist over stuff that doesn't matter. Stuff like this:

1 *"If we don't discuss Q2 today, then all hell will break loose."*

2 *"Can somebody else except me please refill the bloody paper tray???!"*

3 *"Somebody else can turn the printers off tonight – I do it every day."*

4 *"Who's got my mug? It was in the kitchen last time I left it."*

5 *"If I don't get that report by end of play, I'll have to alert HR."*

6 *"Why aren't you wearing the name badges corporate asked us all to wear?"*

7 *"Our profit margin is down 3 per cent – who's to blame?"*

8 "I didn't see you smiling at the office fun day out – you better buck your ideas up if you want to succeed here."

9 "If we don't get that report to corporate by 11am exactly, my head will roll."

10 "If you don't show up to the meeting it makes me look bad."

11 "No one is as busy as me, that's for sure."

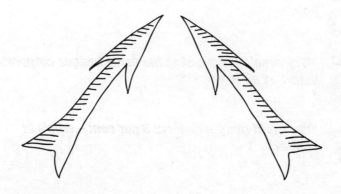

Sicktistics
(Sick Statistics)

In a 2013 poll by the National Sickness Report, it was revealed that employees take an average of 360 days off to sickness in a 45-year career. On average, in the UK, office employees work for 252 days a year and each year 131 million working days are lost due to sickness – eight days per every working man, woman and child in Britain.

Get Awkward #8

Buy a few bottles of multivitamins. You know the ones. Steam off the labels. Create your own label using the title "Smart Pills", and attach the new labels to each new bottle. Now, leave a bottle on each of your co-workers' desks. Every morning, send all your colleagues an email reminding them to take their smart pills today.

Quote Quota #23

> **Your computer needn't be the first thing you see in the morning and the last thing you see at night.**
>
> Simon Mainwaring

Books To Read On The Loo

If you want to spend some quality time away from your desk, may I suggest for your reading pleasure the following epic masterpieces? Should you wish, you could disappear on the toilet for weeks at a time with your eyes feasting on their 700+ pages and your trousers around your ankles.

1. *In Search of Lost Time* by Marcel Proust – 4,215 pages

2. *My Struggle* by Karl Ove Knausgård – 3,600 pages

3. *Atlas Shrugged* by Ayn Rand – 1,957 pages

4. *The Lord of the Rings Trilogy* by J.R.R. Tolkien – 1,137 pages

5. *Infinite Jest* by David Foster Wallace – 1,079 pages

6. *The Recognitions* by William Gaddis – 956 pages

7. *1Q84* by Haruki Murakami – 928 pages

8. *Middlemarch* by George Eliot – 904 pages

9. *Anna Karenina* by Leo Tolstoy – 864 pages

10. *The Goldfinch* by Donna Tartt – 784 pages

Office Camouflage

Do you ever wish you could just blend in and not get noticed, especially when your manager needs something doing urgently, because they can't be bothered to do it themselves? Take a leaf out of the books of these creatures below, ten masters of camouflage:

1. **Chameleon**
2. **Stick insect**
3. **Praying mantis**
4. **Elephant hawk moth**
5. **Leaf insect**
6. **Copperband butterfly fish**
7. **King page butterfly**
8. **Crane fly**
9. **Horned toad**

Quote Quota #97

ff To err is human, but to really foul things up you need a computer. JJ

Paul R. Ehrlich

Top Ten Most Believable Excuses When Calling In Sick

If you want your boss to realistically believe your sickie pleas, then stick with one of these guaranteed* believable excuses:

1 I've got chicken pox (only works once)

2 I've pulled my quada (regular exercisers only)

3 My motorbike/bicycle was stolen this morning (owners of those vehicles only)

4 I've got sunstroke

5 My plane was delayed coming back from X (make sure planes fly to X!)

6 I lost my keys and have to have my locks changed

7 My house has been flooded (Winter use only)

8 My neighbour's cat needs to go to the vet to be put down

9 My child/parent/nephew/uncle needs medical attention

10 My boy/girlfriend developed a rash on their groin that needs checking out

*In no way a guarantee.

Quote Quota #73

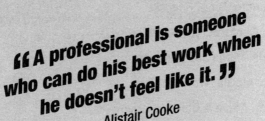

" A professional is someone who can do his best work when he doesn't feel like it. "

Alistair Cooke

Famous Offices In Movies & TV

One of the most successful places to set a film is in the workplace. Nine out of ten* of them revolve around frustrated, bored and unhappy minions rising up against their evil overlords and taking back their lives. Here are Hollywood unhappiest office drones:

1. **Mr. Incredible, *The Incredibles***
2. **Narrator, *Fight Club***
3. **Roy and Moss, *The IT Crowd***
4. **Chandler Bing, *Friends***
5. **Tim Canterbury, *The Office***
6. **Chris, *Parks and Recreation***
7. **Tess McGill, *Working Girl***
8. **Ders, Adam & Blake, *Workaholics***
9. **Michael Bluth, *Arrested Development***
10. **Homer Simpson, *The Simpsons***

*Minions, ironically, is the obvious exception.

Quote Quota #75

FYI

A recent survey reported that one out of three employees who received a promotion in 2015 used a coffee mug with the company logo on it. Quick – find a mug with a logo on – and make sure you hide it where no one, not even yourself, will ever find it.

Get Awkward #9

Buy a bulk order of plain baseball caps online. When they arrive, scribble the word "THINKING CAP" on the front. Now, leave a cap on each of your co-workers' desks. Every morning, remind all your colleagues, via email, to put on their thinking caps today.

Quote Quota #81

" Computers are like Old Testament gods; lots of rules and no mercy. "

Joseph Campbell

Ten Shades Of Brown

Below are the ten shades of brown you're most likely to see in your tea mug – from almost-black sludge to golden brown, norovirus beige to tanned diarrhea. It's amazing how often your slow-witted colleagues will screw up such a simple task:

1. **Beaver – underbrewed**
2. **Beige – too much milk!**
3. **Bole – someone's having a laugh**
4. **Bronze – too orange**
5. **Camel – looking good**
6. **Copper – the perfect "Builder's Brew"**
7. **Fallow – a touch more milk**
8. **Khaki – very anaemic**
9. **Lion – looking good!**
10. **Wheat – somebody hates you**

REMEMBER

If a co-worker brings you a cup of tea that doesn't cut the mustard, or in no way resembles a satisfying hot beverage, resist the urge to give in to instant gratification and stand up and throw it in their face. Instead, spend the rest of the day plotting their very public downfall.

Quote Quota #50

"I think computer viruses should count as life. I think it says something about human nature that the only form of life we have created so far is purely destructive. We've created life in our own image."

Stephen Hawking

Staff Meetings:
Eight Commandments*

You spend most of your working life in meetings. You might as well go prepared. Even if you intend to spare the bare minimum of your brain's CPU to pay attention, take the right precautions, and you can turn the meeting into a great way to score brownie points with the boss – without really trying!

1 Always take a note pad and pen
(to doodle, not take notes)

2 Never stare at your watch
(before the meeting starts, set your iPhone to vibrate silently in your pocket when you want to leave)

3 Never look like you're yawning
(cover it up with a sip of tea by bringing your mug closer to your mouth)

4 Always bring a drink
(gives you a distraction every once in a while)

5 Never look anyone else in the eye
(they'll see the look of sheer boredom in your face)

6 Never interrupt anyone
(it'll look like you are not paying attention)

7 Always be the last to leave the room
(it looks like you care the most)

8 Always tell everyone present, "That was a productive meeting"
(even though it wasn't)

*Do you really need ten?

Quote Quota #82

> **❝ If I had to, I could clean out my desk in five seconds, and nobody would ever know that I'd ever been here. And I'd forget, too. ❞**
>
> Ryan, The Office: An American Workplace

FYI #6

The benefits of a daily dose of coffee are well-known. But what is less known, and was reported in a 2015 survey, is that those who take their coffee black also scored highly on a test that assessed "Machiavellianism", a term used in psychology to describe personalities that are dark, psychopathic, narcissistic and sadistic. In conclusion, those who drink pure black coffee are more likely to express psychopathic tendencies, i.e. are murderers.

How do you drink yours?

Get Awkward #10

Sometimes your co-workers behave like children – throwing tantrums when they don't get their own way, sulking, lashing out, sobbing, etc. If you ever encounter this type of immature behaviour, then the next time they go to lunch, why not replace your colleagues pens with crayons, take away their computer and replace it with a Speak-and-Spell, and leave a pacifier on their desk accompanied by a note, which reads:

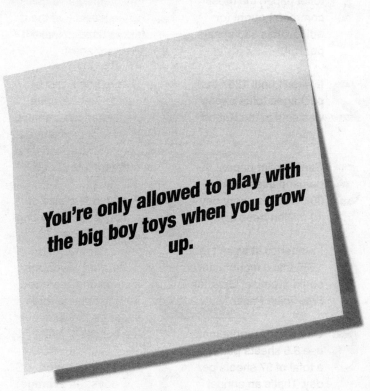

You're only allowed to play with the big boy toys when you grow up.

Toilet Paper Facts

If you're anything like the 37 per cent of office workers who hide in the toilet for up to 45 minutes a day – just sitting there praying for the day to end – then you'll no doubt be hankering for some really good toilet roll facts to keep you "occupied". Today's your lucky day...

1 The cheapest one ply toilet paper, the most common bought for offices, has 333 sheets per roll.

2 It wasn't until 1857 that packaged toilet paper was sold in the United States.

3 Global toilet paper demand uses nearly 30,000 trees every day – 10 million trees a year!

4 In America, it wasn't until 1935 that a manufacturer could promise "Splinter-Free Toilet Paper."

5 On average, consumers use 8.6 sheets per trip – a total of 57 sheets per day. That's an annual total of 20,805 sheets!

6 The reason toilet paper disintegrates so quickly when wet is that the fibers used to make it are very short.

7 On the International Space Station, toilet paper has to be sealed in special containers and compressed. And then dumped into space.

8 The standard size of your grade variety bog paper is 4.5" x 4.5".

9 According to various studies, the average person spends three years on the toilet over the course of a lifetime.

10 The Pentagon, USA, uses, on average, about 666 rolls of toilet paper every day. The same number as the Devil, FYI.

Perfect Tea...For Mugs

1 **Do not turn your back on the kettle when boiling tea**
(Wait until the kettle is fully boiled. There is a clicking noise, six seconds after the kettle has fully boiled. Once this occurs, you can take the kettle off. Never before.)

2 **Do not brew the tea for less than three minutes**
(If you do, the tea will be scorched and the flavour will be diminished.)

3 **Do not leave the teabag in the mug**
(You're not an animal.)

4 **Never take sugar in your tea**
(You're sweet enough.)

Feel free to photocopy the following pages and use them as your To Do List for the coming week. Remember, none of things you write down should be work-related!

>>> *Monday* <<<

☐ ....

☐ ....

☐ ....

☐ ....

☐ ....

☐ ....

☐ ....

☐ ....

☐ ....

>>> *Tuesday* <<<

- [ ] ....
- [ ] ....
- [ ] ....
- [ ] ....
- [ ] ....
- [ ] ....
- [ ] ....
- [ ] ....
- [ ] ....
- [ ] ....
- [ ] ....

>>> *Wednesday* <<<

- [ ] ....
- [ ] ....
- [ ] ....
- [ ] ....
- [ ] ....
- [ ] ....
- [ ] ....
- [ ] ....
- [ ] ....
- [ ] ....
- [ ] ....

>>> Thursday <<<

>>> *Friday* <<<

- [ ] ....
- [ ] ....
- [ ] ....
- [ ] ....
- [ ] ....
- [ ] ....
- [ ] ....
- [ ] ....
- [ ] ....
- [ ] ....
- [ ] ....

Rip This Page Out

(It'll make you feel better.)